## At Issue

# What Is the Impact of Green Practices?

# Other Books in the At Issue Series

# At Issue

# What Is the Impact of Green Practices?

*Tamara Thompson, Book Editor*

**GREENHAVEN PRESS**
*A part of Gale, Cengage Learning*

GALE
CENGAGE Learning®

Farmington Hills, Mich • San Francisco • New York • Waterville, Maine
Meriden, Conn • Mason, Ohio • Chicago

Judy Galens, *Manager, Frontlist Acquisitions*

*For more information, contact:*
Greenhaven Press
27500 Drake Rd.
Farmington Hills, MI 48331-3535
Or you can visit our Internet site at gale.cengage.com

**LIBRARY OF CONGRESS CATALOGING-IN-PUBLICATION DATA**

Names: Thompson, Tamara, editor.
Title: What is the impact of green practices? / Tamara Thompson, book editor.
Description: Farmington Hills, Mich : Greenhaven Press, a part of Gale, Cengage Learning, [2016] | Series: At issue | Includes bibliographical references and index.
Identifiers: LCCN 2015031226 | ISBN 9780737774146 (hardcover) | ISBN 9780737774153 (pbk.)
Subjects: LCSH: Green movement. | Environmental responsibility. | Human ecology.
Classification: LCC GE195 .W49 2016 | DDC 363.7--dc23
LC record available at http://lccn.loc.gov/2015031226

Printed in the United States of America
1 2 3 4 5        20 19 18 17 16

# Contents

# Introduction

Consumers have long been encouraged to reduce, reuse, and recycle, but environmental awareness has come a long way since the first Earth Day celebration in 1970. Climate change is now a top global concern and being "green" has become a mainstream way of thinking—and living—for millions of people.

One key goal of a green lifestyle is to reduce the volume of greenhouse gasses that contribute to global warming by reducing one's own "carbon footprint," the sum total of all carbon emissions produced in the course of one's activities and product consumption.

According to the Fifth Annual Tork Sustainability Study by Harris Interactive, some 78 percent of American consumers say they buy green products and services, citing concerns about health and the environment as their main reasons for doing so.

"We've gone far beyond the hybrid car to arrive at organic unbleached cotton T-shirts, bamboo bed linens and biodegradable to-go drink lids. You can 'green up' your computer with nontoxic flash drives and go the extra mile to buy an Energy Star washing machine instead of the old power-guzzling one,"[1] writes Julia Layton for the website How Stuff Works. Layton goes on to note that "the expanding trend toward green consumerism indicates, at the very least, widespread recognition that the planet is in trouble, and some sort of intention to do something about it—however small that something may be."[2]

1. Julia Layton, "Is Green Consumerism a Contradiction?," How Stuff Works, accessed July 14, 2015. http://science.howstuffworks.com/environmental/green-science/green-consumerism-contradiction.htm.
2. Ibid.

But does it really make a difference to practice the so-called three R's—reduce, reuse, recycle? To take public transportation, drive an electric car, or bike to work? To shop for green products, choose natural cleaning supplies, or use reusable grocery bags? To build environmentally friendly buildings, develop alternative clean energy sources, or buy carbon offsets to make up for the pollution that our actions contribute to the environment?

It's maddeningly hard to say.

Quantifying the impact of many green practices is difficult or impossible, largely because there is little good empirical data, but also because nothing happens in a bubble and unanticipated consequences sometimes occur from even the most benign and well-intentioned efforts.

For example, one might reasonably expect that having clean energy sources such as solar or wind as part of a local utility's power mix would reduce carbon emissions from the utility, but it doesn't. Energy-efficient technologies, it turns out, promote higher consumption by consumers, a rebound effect that offsets the carbon benefits of solar and wind technologies.

Indeed, the same principle holds true elsewhere in the green consumer economy, where the availability of eco-friendly choices serves to fuel ever-more green consumption. When consumers have access to sustainable seafood, they justify eating more of it; when they buy recycled paper towels, they reach for them more often; when they have fuel-efficient vehicles, they drive further and more frequently; and when they have easy access to recycling programs, they consume more products that come in cans and bottles.

"We can't shop the planet green, no matter how much we might want to believe it," observes Guy Pearse in his 2014 book, *The Greenwash Effect*. "The savings from the relatively small number of green products being sold are swamped by production growth due to dramatic increases in sales volumes."[3]

In addition to the rebound effect (also called the Jevons paradox), there are sometimes other unanticipated consequences that come along with acts that are intended to benefit the environment. For example, many communities have banned plastic shopping bags in stores to help cut down on litter and keep wildlife from ingesting the notoriously problematic plastic material. But consumers who switch to reusable bags seldom wash them; reusable totes have been linked to food poisoning and the presence of harmful bacteria, an altogether unanticipated side-effect of a well-intentioned green initiative.

Similarly, the Energy Independence and Security Act of 2007 mandated the phase-out of incandescent light bulbs in the United States in favor of compact florescent bulbs, which work up to fifteen times longer and use as little as half the energy. It was estimated that replacing all the incandescent bulbs in the United States with compact florescent ones would save 80 terrawatt hours (TWh) of electricity each year, nearly 2 percent of total US energy use in 2013. If incandescent bulbs were replaced worldwide, it would save some 409 TWh, some 2.5 percent of total global energy. That translates to millions of tons less carbon dioxide emitted into the atmosphere, a not-insignificant reduction in greenhouse gas emissions.

But the widely adopted new bulbs emit ultraviolet rays that are harmful to humans, and they also contain the toxic element mercury, which must be carefully handled and properly disposed of as hazardous waste. Although they have helped reduce global $CO_2$ emissions as promised, compact florescents have created an entirely new environmental problem because they expose consumers to dangerous mercury when they break and the majority of used bulbs end up in

3. Guy Pearse, *The Greenwash Effect*. New York: Skyhorse, 2014, p. 244.

landfills, where they can leach mercury into the soil and water, rather than being properly recycled.

Complexities like these underscore the difficulty in trying to determine whether a green practice will ultimately be good for the environment, but some say it's no reason to stop trying.

"None of this means we should stop buying—or stop buying the greener product," writes Pearse, "but it does mean we need to be realistic . . . about the impact that our purchases make."[4]

Others disagree and insist that consumption itself—whether green or otherwise—remains the root of the problem: "The assumption that by buying anything, whether green or not, we're solving the problem is a misperception," environmental author and organic farmer Michael Ableman told *The New York Times*. "Consuming is a significant part of the problem to begin with. Maybe the solution is instead of buying five pairs of organic cotton jeans, buy one pair of regular jeans instead."[5]

The authors in *At Issue: What Is the Impact of Green Practices?* present a wide array of viewpoints that consider the benefits and unintended consequences of a variety of green practices.

4. Ibid., p. 245.
5. Quoted in Alex Williams, "Buying Into the Green Movement," *New York Times*, July 1, 2007. http://www.nytimes.com/2007/07/01/fashion/01green.html?ex&_r=0.

1

# Recycling Programs Divert Tons of Material from Landfills Every Year

*US Environmental Protection Agency*

*The US Environmental Protection Agency (EPA) is the federal government agency charged with ensuring that both human and environmental health in the United States are protected and preserved. The EPA writes and enforces regulations based on laws passed by Congress and works to influence and promote positive environmental stewardship and policies.*

*Americans produce a massive amount of waste each year, but recycling programs have significantly reduced the amount of trash destined for landfills. In 2013, the most recent year for which figures were available, more than 34 percent of US waste was recycled, including more than 87 million tons of paper, yard trimmings, aluminum, electronics, plastics, and glass. Lead-acid batteries are the most recycled material, with a 99 percent recycling rate, while steel cans have reached the 70.6 percent mark. Using recycled materials to make things is good for the environment and also saves both money and energy.*

Our trash, or MSW [municipal solid waste], is comprised of various items Americans commonly throw away after being used. These items include packaging, food, grass clippings, sofas, computers, tires and refrigerators. MSW does not include industrial, hazardous or construction waste.

US Environmental Protection Agency, "Advancing Sustainable Materials Management: 2013 Fact Sheet," June 2015.

## Rising Recycling Rates

In 2013, Americans recovered over 64.7 million tons of MSW through recycling, and over 22 million tons through composting. This is 1.12 pounds per person per day for recycling and 0.39 pounds per person per day for composting. Americans combusted about 32.7 million tons (about 13 percent) for energy recovery. Subtracting out what is recycled and composted, we combusted (with energy recovery) or discarded in landfills 2.89 pounds per person per day of MSW.

---

*Containers and packaging make up the largest portion of MSW generated: 29.8 percent, or over 75 million tons.*

---

In 2013, the rate of lead-acid battery recovery was about 99 percent (2.85 million tons). The rate of newspapers/mechanical papers recovery was about 67 percent (5.4 million tons), and over 60 percent (20.6 million tons) of yard trimmings were recovered. About 134.3 million tons of MSW (52.8 percent) were discarded in landfills in 2013.

Three materials whose recycling rates rose from 2012 to 2013 are yard trimmings, selected consumer electronics and food. In 2013, the rate of yard trimmings composting was 60.2 percent (20.60 million tons), up from 57.7 percent (19.59 million tons). This translates to 130 pounds per person per year of yard trimmings composted in 2013. In 2013, the rate of selected consumer electronics recovery was 40.4 percent (1.27 million tons) up from 30.6 percent in 2012 (1.00 million tons). This translates to 8 pounds per person per year recovered in 2013. In 2013, the rate of food recovery was 5.0 percent (1.84 million tons), up from 4.8 percent in 2012 (1.74 million tons). This translates to 12 pounds per person per year composted in 2013. Over the last few years, EPA [Environmental Protection Agency] has been heavily invested in these areas.

## Products in MSW

The breakdown of the 254 million tons of MSW generated in 2013 by product category follows. Containers and packaging make up the largest portion of MSW generated: 29.8 percent, or over 75 million tons. Nondurable and durable goods each make up about 20.3 percent (over 51 million tons). Food makes up 14.6 percent (37 million tons), yard trimmings make up 13.5 percent (34 million tons) and other wastes make up 1.5 percent (4 million tons)....

Paper products, steel and aluminum were the most recycled materials by percentage in this category. Over 75 percent of paper and paperboard containers and packaging was recycled. Over 72 percent of steel packaging (mostly cans) was recycled. The recycling rate for aluminum packaging was almost 39 percent, including over 55 percent of aluminum beverage cans.

Thirty-four percent of glass containers were recycled, while over 26 percent of wood packaging (mostly wood pallets) was recovered. Over 14 percent of plastic containers and packaging were recycled—mostly from soft drink, milk and water bottles. Plastic bottles were the most recycled plastic products. Polyethylene terephthalate (PET) bottles and jars were recovered at over 31 percent. Recovery of high density polyethylene (HDPE) natural (white translucent) bottles was also estimated at over 28 percent.

Overall recovery of nondurable goods was about 32 percent in 2013. Nondurable goods generally last less than three years. Newspapers/mechanical papers and other paper products were the most recycled nondurable goods. Newspapers/mechanical papers include newspapers, directories, inserts, and some advertisement and direct mail printing. Sixty-seven percent of newspapers/mechanical papers were recovered. Collectively, the recovery of other paper products such as office paper and magazines was over 41 percent in 2013. Clothing, footwear and other textile products are included in the nondurable goods category. These products were recovered for recycling at a rate of over 16 percent.

Overall, 18 percent of durable goods was recovered in 2013. Due to the high rate of lead recovery from lead-acid batteries, nonferrous metals (other than aluminum) had one of the highest recovery rates. With an almost 99 percent recycling rate, lead-acid batteries continued to be one of the most recovered products. Recovery of steel in all durable goods was about 27 percent, with high rates of recovery from appliances and other miscellaneous items. Recovery of selected consumer electronics was about 40 percent.

---

*Recycling has environmental benefits at every stage in the life cycle of a consumer product.*

---

Measured by percentage of generation, products with the highest recovery rates in 2013 were lead-acid batteries (99 percent), corrugated boxes (88.5 percent), steel cans (70.6 percent), newspapers/mechanical papers (67.0 percent), yard trimmings (60.2 percent), major appliances (58.6 percent), aluminum cans (55.1 percent), mixed paper (41.3 percent), tires (40.5 percent) and selected consumer electronics (40.4 percent).

## The Benefits of Recycling

Recycling has environmental benefits at every stage in the life cycle of a consumer product—from the raw material with which it's made to its final method of disposal. By utilizing used, unwanted or obsolete materials as industrial feedstocks, or for new materials or products, Americans can each do their part to make recycling—including composting—work. Aside from reducing GHG emissions, which contribute to global warming, recycling (including composting) also provides significant economic and job creation impacts....

In 2013, Americans recycled and composted over 87 million tons of MSW. This provides an annual reduction of more than 186 million metric tons of carbon dioxide equivalent emissions, comparable to removing the emissions from over 39 million passenger vehicles from the road in one year.

## MSW Generation and Household Spending

Over the years, the change in the amount of MSW generated typically imitated trends in how much money American households spend on goods and services. Personal Consumer Expenditures (PCE) measure US household spending on goods and services such as food, clothing, vehicles and recreation services. PCE accounts for approximately 70 percent of US Gross Domestic Product [GDP], a key indicator of economic growth. PCE adjusted for inflation is referred to as real PCE. This is a more useful metric in making comparisons over time because it normalizes the value of a dollar by considering how much a dollar could purchase in the past versus today....

[R]eal PCE has increased at a faster rate than MSW generation, and the disparity has become even more distinct since the mid-1990s. This indicates the amount of MSW generated per dollar spent is falling. In other words, America's economy has been able to enjoy dramatic increases in household spending on consumer goods and services without this being at the expense of the societal impact of similarly increasing MSW generation rates. This figure also shows that the MSW generated per capita leveled off in the early-to-mid 2000s and has since fallen. This is important because as population continues to grow, it will be necessary for MSW generated per capita to continue to fall to maintain or decrease the total amount of MSW generated as a country.

# 2

# Recycling Benefits the Economy and Creates Jobs

*Neil Seldman*

*Neil Seldman is president of the Institute for Local Self-Reliance in Washington, DC, a nonprofit advocacy group that helps communities find local solutions for sustainable development.*

*The US recycling industry has generated more than a million jobs—a figure that is expected to double as the demand for recycled materials continues to grow in the industrial and agricultural sectors. A wide variety of recycling, refurbishing, and repurposing programs across the country not only create jobs but also save taxpayers money and generate other significant economic benefits for local communities. One in particular, the privately owned building-materials salvage company Urban Ore in Berkeley, California, has redefined what is possible in the reclamation industry and has become a model for reuse stores around the world.*

In the late 1960s and early 1970s, the U.S. recycling movement benefitted from the decentralized nature of our government. With 10,000 local governments each in charge of their own solid waste, it was possible for experimentation and sharing successful approaches across the country. Today in the midst of the Great Recession [2012], decentralized recycling is proving its worth to the country once again. The recycling industry has created well over 1 million jobs and is projected to add another million jobs as recycling levels continue to divert more and more material to industry and agriculture. The level of experimentation continues. The following stories introduce just a fraction of the new job creating and job sustaining endeavors from around the U.S.

In Bridgeport, Connecticut, a mattress recycling and refurbishing enterprise started up in late June [2012]. Twenty workers will process 100,000 mattresses and box springs annually. This will reduce transfer station and landfill costs, while making good end products available to consumers at pennies on the dollar compared to new mattresses from formal retail stores. The plant is owned by the Greater Bridgeport Community Development Corporation, which used a $100,000 Community Development Block Grant (CDBG) to leverage additional capital.

---

*Austin [Texas] just released an extraordinary business plan for resource recovery that will guide the city to 90 percent diversion of discarded materials by 2020.*

---

## Model Programs

An array of refurbishing operations in Eugene, Oregon—including mattresses, automobiles, appliances, computers and furniture—sell through 11 outlet stores run by Saint Vincent de Paul (SVDP). It is estimated these operations have helped lower the cost of living in Eugene by 3 percent. SVDP's total operations employ over 400 workers at living wages plus health insurance. SVDP also manufacturers products made from window glass and fire starters made from old crayons. Since the great recession of 2008, SVDP has hired over 100 new workers and raised wages.

In Reading, Pennsylvania, the new administration has hired its own workers at union wage and benefit levels to manage the city's recycling program. There are 10 new jobs and the city is expecting to save $300,000. Further, by controlling its own materials, Reading can direct these resources to companies that will locate manufacturing plants in the city. Reading will be the site of the first U.S. plant that uses 40 tons/day recycled high grade paper and recycled cotton to produce stationery, copy paper, envelopes and file folders for local and regional markets. The Greys Paper Recycling Industries plant will create 100 jobs at $14/hour, plus an additional 20 jobs in distribution and warehousing.

United Community Services, the city's workforce development agent, will identify, screen and recruit workers. Mayor Vaughn Spencer is introducing additional creative ways to use raw available materials for sustainable economic growth.

In Alachua County, Florida, a 40-acre Resource Recovery Park has been created for recycling and composting companies. Similarly, an industrial park for these types of companies is being developed in Austin, Texas. Austin just released an extraordinary business plan for resource recovery that will guide the city to 90 percent diversion of discarded materials by 2020. The report will save cities seeking to replicate these goals hundreds of thousands of dollars in consulting fees.

---

*Urban Ore has served as a model for large and small reuse stores all over the world.*

---

## Urban Agriculture

In Poughkeepsie, New York, the city is providing 4 acres to Greenway, Inc., a composting company, which will create the foundation for an intensive urban agriculture sector. Urban agriculture is essential for sustainable cities. David Crockett, director of the Office of Sustainability in Chattanooga, reports that if just 10 percent of the food eaten in the city were grown in the city, it would make a $1 billion impact on the local economy.

In Atlanta, urban agriculture is making considerable progress. Biponica, Inc. has produced two grow facilities at Park Department outdoor centers which grow fish using algae and duck weed as feed, and vegetables from the nutrients in fish excretions. Elemental Impact has established the downtown Zero Waste Zone to segregate organic waste for composting. This also makes it easier to recycle nonorganic discarded materials. Elemental Impact is also working with the city's airport, the busiest in the U.S., to capture back of the house and concourse organic waste, as well as the plastic packages used to deliver food to the facility. Elemental Impact is now working closely with the National Restaurant Association to establish these zones in many U.S. cities.

## Reuse and Niche Recycling

Also in Atlanta, the faith-based organization Charitable Connections has recently expanded the Fuller Center, its restore that distributes used and new building materials to low-income customers. Charitable Connections also has established a recycled paint enterprise, as well as attracted an electronic scrap recycling company and a textile recycling company to the community.

In Berkeley, California, Urban Ore has served as a model for large and small reuse stores all over the world. The privately owned enterprise started in 1979 at the tipping face of the old Berkeley landfill, and recovered its first round of tools and equipment from the landfill itself. Incorporated as a Subchapter S corporation in 1980, Urban Ore is open 360 days a year, 10 hours a day. Conducting business under the motto "to end the age of waste," Urban Ore's staff diverts used building materials and other products from landfills and transfer stations by sorting, cleaning, organizing and selling products to individual customers and other reuse stores in the San Francisco Bay Area. It recovers reusable goods by scavenging under contracts from municipally-owned transfer stations in Berkeley and El Cerrito.

## A Whole New Designation

In 1999, Urban Ore had to rewrite Berkeley's zoning law to be able to move across town onto the property it subsequently bought. With the cooperation of the Planning Department and the blessing of the City Council at the time, a new category of conservation business that can occupy Mixed Use/Light Industrial properties "as of right" was created. That designation is Materials Recovery Enterprise.

The enterprise now has 38 workers and grosses over $2.6 million annually. Recovered materials that cannot be sold are recycled. Urban Ore sends to landfill less than 2 percent of the 7,000 to 8,000 tons of materials and products that come its way each year. It was able to purchase most of its 3.2-acre facility in West Berkeley in 2009, with loans from the Small Business Administration, a local bank, and the Alameda County Source Reduction and Recycling Board. The company has a design service that has helped around 30 private industry and local governments in the U.S. and other countries to develop transfer stations that maximize recovery from businesses, haulers and individuals. Learn more at urbanore.com.

# 3

# Recycling Is a Waste of Time, Money, and Energy

*Edwin Decker*

*Freelance journalist Edwin Decker is a regular contributor to the* City Beat *newsweekly in San Diego and host of the popular podcast* Sordid Tales.

*The idea that recycling is necessary is based on fallacies and faulty premises. First, it is simply untrue that landfill space is filling up; there is currently plenty of room for the waste Americans produce and then still plenty more room for landfill expansion. Recycling also does not save money; curbside recycling costs significantly more than it does to dump waste in a landfill. On balance, recycling isn't even beneficial to the planet because of all the carbon-intensive resources—such as garbage trucks and industrial recycling plants—that are used to facilitate the process from start to finish. Recycling is a feel-good bandwagon that simply isn't worth it.*

As a fence-sitting political independent, I've taken a lot of grief over the years from my mostly Democratic friends who say it's a copout to avoid picking a side. And while I adore the progressive attitude of the Democratic Party, celebrate its alliance with intellectualism and get all weepy over its institutional empathy for the underdog, the truth is, liberalism—when left unchecked—will go from zero to shitty in 60 seconds.

When a problem is identified, liberals tend to lurch into action. This is a noble (yet dangerous) instinct, and woe be the sorry sap who gets in the way of the Rebel-beral with a Cause. Indeed, I can think of no better example than curbside recycling.

The reasons for recycling, we're told, is that it's good for the environment and saves money and we're running out of landfill space. And anyone who doesn't agree with this must hate the planet and want to kill Bambi. Well color me a Bambivore, because it's all deer shit.

---

*As for the other proposed reasons for recycling, that it saves money and is good for the environment, there are a lot of smart, informed people who say that it does neither.*

---

For the most part, the hysteria over diminishing landfill space erupted in 1989 when J. Winston Porter, then an administrator for the Environmental Protection Agency (EPA), wrote a report saying that America was running out of places to put its trash. Porter's egregiously incorrect conclusion was based on the fact that nearly 3,000 landfills had shut down between 1982 and 1987. However, had he performed even the slightest bit of research, he'd have learned that, while the number of landfills had decreased, the size of each of the remaining fills had increased—by, on average, 20 times.

## The Landfill-Space Fallacy

In a phone interview, Jim Thompson, president of the *Waste Business Journal*, explained that in the early '80s, most of the country's 6,000 or 7,000 landfills were run by small, unregulated municipalities. Many of these facilities had to shut down due to increasing restrictions: Landfills may not be located near groundwater, the lining system must be a multilayered combination of impermeable clay, gravel, sheeting and drainage; the methane gas must be either flared off or recycled periodically. These regulations forced many of the smaller operations out of business, and they were replaced by corporate "mega-landfills" that could afford all the retrofits and other legal requirements. The point is, there was, and is, no shortage of landfill space, and even Porter—now president of the Waste Policy Center, a consultancy firm for businesses and government agencies—has backed away from that claim.

As for the other proposed reasons for recycling, that it saves money and is good for the environment, there are a lot of smart, informed people who say that it does neither. Using data provided by Franklin Associates (an EPA-sanctioned waste consulting firm), Daniel K. Benjamin (author of *The 8 Great Myths of Recycling*) reported that "overall curbside recycling costs run between 35 and 55 percent higher than the [landfill] option."

Even the voraciously pro-curbside-recycling Porter reported (on the "Recycling" episode of the Showtime series, *Bullshit!*) that it costs local governments an average of $150 per ton to recycle, but only $50 or $60 a ton to dump it in a landfill.

## Worth the Price?

But, hey, if it's good for the planet, it's worth the price, right? Well, sure, it would be—if it weren't that the whole recycling operation is, in itself, just another pumping, smoking, leaking, spewing, spilling, poisoning, polluting mega-machine. Forget about all those extra, specialized recycling trucks (which use more fuel and emit more carbon dioxide); forget about all the leaflets and other mailing materials used to inform the public about correct recycling behavior; forget about the added manpower and its carbon footprint—recycling plants pollute as much as any manufacturing plant, maybe worse because they use acids, colorants, stabilizers, retardants and lubricants during processing, causing a runoff sludge more noxious than [grunge rocker] Courtney Love's radioactive douchebag magma.

Now, it could be argued, as Jim Thompson did, that recycling could be viable someday and may not be a waste of time and money. Perhaps. Certainly reasonable minds can disagree. My point is: Why were the pros and cons not thoroughly discussed before the blue bins started showing up? Why didn't we listen to The Borg [from *Star Trek*] when they said, "Recycling is futile"? They should know. They're The Borg!

The whole thing reminds me of the No Nukes campaign of the 1970s. Somehow we were led to believe that nuclear power and nuclear bombs posed the same threat. If you disagreed, you were branded a lover of radiation sickness. So they stopped building nuclear plants. However, had an intelligent discussion played out at the time, we'd have learned that nuclear power is the safest, most efficient and most environmentally friendly of all the energy options, and if we continued making newer and better nuclear plants back then, we might not be having so many energy problems today.

This is why I can't fully sign on to the liberal worldview. This is why, for all its buffoonery and bigotry, we still need conservatism to keep progressivism on a leash. This is why I remain, ever so proudly, in the middle, where rational people realize the world is too complex to see problems through partisan eyes.

# 4

# Studies Link Reusable Grocery Bags to Foodborne Illnesses and Theft

*Steve Holt*

*Steve Holt is a freelance writer who regularly contributes to* TakePart, *an online news magazine and social activism community. He also writes about food for the* Boston Globe *and other publications.*

*Reusable grocery bags have become popular—or even mandatory—in many communities nationwide, but there is a potential danger to using them. Experts say reusable bags can harbor bacteria, such as E. coli, that can cause serious foodborne illnesses. A recent study of reusable bags found that more than half of the bags tested were contaminated with some sort of bacteria. Although healthy people aren't likely to get sick from most of the bacteria found, it is a good reason to wash reusable grocery bags regularly. Additionally, evidence suggests that grocery theft has increased in areas where plastic bags are banned and consumers must supply their own.*

When Americans need to get groceries, a growing number of us have grown accustomed to grabbing a stack of reusable bags and forgoing plastic at the checkout line. Some municipalities have even banned plastic bags altogether.

And since bag bans remove plastic that would normally end up in landfills or in the stomachs of sea turtles, it's a great idea, right?

Not so fast. Some, including a few scientists, are saying that these reusable bags are cesspools for bacteria, including the feared E. coli strain, and that bag bans send more Americans to the hospital with food poisoning. In a paper titled "Grocery Bag Bans and Foodborne Illness," Jonathan Klick and Joshua D. Wright, from the University of Pennsylvania Institute for Law and Economics, point to what they say is a "46 percent increase in the deaths from foodborne illnesses" in San Francisco since the city banned the distribution of plastic bags in 2007.

The paper, published last November [2012], summarizes research analyzing the bacterial content in a sampling of reusable grocery bags, finding high levels of E. coli and other bacteria. Then, analyzing emergency room admissions related to bacterial intestinal infections in San Francisco County since the 2007 ban, the authors found that ER admissions appeared to increase by at least 25 percent relative to other California counties.

## Undue Concern?

Immediately, headlines began to pop up criticizing, or at least questioning, bans on plastic bags, and it seemed opponents of environmental causes finally had some ammunition in their camp.

---

*In 2010, a study [by the American Chemistry Council] ... discovered the presence of microbes in tests on 84 reusable grocery bags from shoppers in California and Arizona.*

---

But last month [February 2013], epidemiologist and Health Officer for San Francisco Tomás Arágon struck back, calling the connection Klick and Wright made between the city's bag ban and foodborne illness unfounded. He wrote that he'd received a "flurry of concerned calls" following the release of the report, so his team looked into it.

"Based on our review of this paper, and our disease surveillance and death registry data," he wrote in a memo countering the bag ban criticism, "the Klick and Wright's conclusion that San Francisco's policy of banning of plastic bags has caused a significant increase in gastrointestinal bacterial infections and a '46 percent increase in the deaths from foodborne illnesses' is not warranted."

In 2010, a study funded by the American Chemistry Council (which, incidentally, makes a number of these reusable bags) discovered the presence of microbes in tests on 84 reusable grocery bags from shoppers in California and Arizona. More than half the bags contained some sort of coliform bacteria, a category that includes *Escherichia coli*.

What the study didn't identify, however, were the specific strains of E. coli found in the bags, and Dr. Susan Fernyak, director of San Francisco's Communicable Disease and Control Prevention division, believes there was never any risk of widespread, or even isolated, sickness.

"Your average healthy person is not going to get sick from the bacteria that were listed," she told NPR [National Public Radio].

The solution, say many, is not to repeal bag bans, but to encourage shoppers to wash their reusable bags more often. The Klick and Wright study found that 97 percent of those surveyed never wash their reusable bags.

## What About Theft?

But safety aside, do reusable bags lead to an increase in theft? One Seattle grocery store owner thinks so. Since the city banned plastic bags last summer, he told the *Seattle Post-Intelligencer* that he's lost at least $5,000 in produce and between $3,000 and $4,000 in frozen food. "We've never lost that much before," [he] said.

Theft may actually be a bigger problem facing the reusable bag trend than the food safety issue. The problem, say store owners, is that the reusable bags more easily conceal items thieves don't intend to pay for. Twenty-one percent of Seattle business owners say they've seen increased theft since the city started banning bags, according to data released in January by Seattle Public Utilities.

Whether or not reusable bags increase food poisoning and theft, one has to think that these are growing pains for a small lifestyle change that makes a big difference to the living creatures in our oceans—and our planet as a whole.

5

# Water Conservation Practices Benefit Communities Nationwide

*US Environmental Protection Agency*

*The US Environmental Protection Agency (EPA) is the federal government agency charged with ensuring that both human and environmental health in the United States are protected and preserved. The EPA writes and enforces regulations based on laws passed by Congress and works to influence and promote positive environmental stewardship and policies.*

*Communities nationwide are adopting water conservation practices that make a difference, and there are many things that consumers can do to reduce their water use. If everyone in the country switched to high-efficiency toilets, for example, it could save nearly two billion gallons of water per day nationwide. "WaterSense" certified efficient appliances, such as washing machines, dishwashers, and water heaters, are also reducing both water and energy use, hence reducing greenhouse gas emissions that promote climate change. Landscaping is another big area of water consumption and there are a variety of strategies that can reduce waste. When it comes to water, using less is more.*

Did you know that less than 1% of all the water on Earth can be used by people? The rest is salt water (the kind you find in the ocean) or is frozen. Communities across the country are starting to face challenges in maintaining healthy

US Environmental Protection Agency, "Conserving Water," epa.gov, April 24, 2014.

and affordable water supplies; that's why it's more important than ever to use our water wisely and not waste it. In addition, it takes large amounts of energy to produce and transport clean water and to process waste water.

A typical household uses approximately 260 gallons of water every day. We can reduce this amount and save money by using water more efficiently—detecting and fixing leaky faucets, installing high efficiency clothes washers and toilets, and watering the lawn and garden with the minimum amount of water needed.

Most of us know we can save water if we turn off the tap while brushing our teeth (as much as 3,000 gallons per year!), but did you know that there are products that will help save water when the tap is on? WaterSense and ENERGYSTAR®, programs sponsored by EPA, have identified high-performance, water-efficient appliances, fixtures, water systems, and accessories that reduce water use in the home and help preserve the nation's water resources. By saving water, you also save energy; the [programs are] discussed in detail here.

---

*Toilets are by far the main source of water use in the home, accounting for nearly 30 percent of residential indoor water consumption.*

---

WaterSense, a partnership program sponsored by EPA, seeks to protect the future of our nation's water supply by promoting water efficiency and enhancing the market for water-efficient products, programs, and practices.

As communities across the country begin facing challenges regarding water supply and water infrastructure, WaterSense can help consumers identify water-efficient products and programs. The WaterSense label tells the consumer that products and programs that carry the label meet water efficiency and performance criteria, and will help save water, money, and energy.

## Toilets Are Water Hogs

Toilets are by far the main source of water use in the home, accounting for nearly 30 percent of residential indoor water consumption. Toilets also happen to be a major source of wasted water due to leaks and inefficiency.

Older toilets, manufactured before 1992 when the Energy Policy Act mandated water efficient toilets, use up to 3.5 gallons per flush. Replacing these toilets with WaterSense labeled toilets could save nearly 2 billion gallons per day across the country. Switching to high-efficiency toilets can save a family of four, on average, $2,000 in water bills over the lifetime of the toilets. There are a number of high-efficiency toilet options, including dual flush technology. Dual flush toilets have two flush volumes—a full flush for solids and a reduced flush for liquids only. Whether you're remodeling a bathroom, building a new home, or simply replacing an old, leaky toilet, a WaterSense labeled toilet is a high-performing, water-efficient option worth considering.

Composting toilets are another option for those who want to be very green. Composting toilets have been an established technology for more than 30 years, and recent advances have made them easy to use and similar in look and feel to regular toilets. As they require little to no water, composting toilet systems can provide a solution to sanitation and environmental problems in unsewered, rural, and suburban areas.

## Faucets and Showerheads

Faucets account for more than 15 percent of indoor household water use—more than 1 trillion gallons of water across the United States each year. WaterSense labeled bathroom sink faucets and accessories can reduce a sink's water flow by 30 percent or more without sacrificing performance. If every household in the United States installed WaterSense labeled bathroom sink faucets or faucet accessories, we could save more than $350 million in water utility bills and more than

60 billion gallons of water annually—enough to meet public water demand in a city the size of Miami for more than 150 days!

If you are not in the market for a new faucet, consider replacing the aerator in your older faucet with a more efficient one. The aerator—the screw-on tip of the faucet—ultimately determines the maximum flow rate of a faucet. Aerators are inexpensive to replace and are an effective water-efficiency measure.

Also keep in mind that you can significantly reduce water use by simply repairing leaks in fixtures—toilets, faucets, and showerheads—or pipes.

---

*You can reduce your monthly water heating bills by selecting the appropriate water heater for your home or pool . . . and by using some energy-efficient water heating strategies.*

---

Showering accounts for approximately 17 percent of residential indoor water use in the United States—more than 1.2 trillion gallons of water consumed each year. You can purchase quality, high-efficiency shower fixtures for around $10 to $20 a piece and achieve water savings of 25-60 percent. Select a high-efficiency showerhead with a flow rate of less than 2.5 gpm (gallons per minute) for maximum water efficiency. Before 1992, some showerheads had flow rates of 5.5 gpm, so you might want to replace older models if you're not sure of the flow rate.

## Appliances

If all U.S. households installed water-efficient appliances, the country would save more than 3 trillion gallons of water and more than $18 billion dollars per year! For instance, the average washing machine uses about 41 gallons of water per load, and is the second largest water user in your home. High-efficiency washing machines use 35 to 50 percent less water, as well as 50 percent less energy per load. If you are in the market for a new dishwasher or clothes washer, consider buying an efficient, water-saving ENERGY STAR® model to reduce water and energy use. To save more water, look for a clothes washer with a low water factor. A water factor is the number of gallons per cycle per cubic foot that a clothes washer uses. So, if a washer uses 18 gallons per cycle and has a tub volume of 3.0 cubic feet, then the water factor is 6.0. The lower the water factor, the more efficient the washer is.

## Hot Water Systems

Water heating is the third largest energy expense in your home. It typically accounts for about 13% of your utility bill, and can account for 14%–25% of the energy consumed in your home. You can reduce your monthly water heating bills by selecting the appropriate water heater for your home or pool—such as tankless, heat pump, or solar hot water heaters—and by using some energy-efficient water heating strategies.

If your water heater's tank leaks, you may need a new water heater. If you are not in the market for a new hot water heater, consider installing an insulation blanket on your water heater tank, and insulate at least the first 3 to 6 feet of the hot and cold water pipes connected to the water heater. When installing a hot water heater insulation blanket:

- For electric hot-water storage tanks, be careful not to cover the thermostat.

- For natural gas or oil hot-water storage tanks, be careful not to cover the water heater's top, bottom, thermostat, or burner compartment.

- Always make sure to follow the manufacturer's recommendations.

These strategies will help get hot water to you faster, saving thousands of gallons of water per year in each household.

## Landscaping and Irrigation

Of the 26 billion gallons of water consumed daily in the United States, approximately 7.8 billion gallons, or 30 percent, is devoted to outdoor uses. The majority of this is used for irrigation. In the summer, the amount of water used outdoors by a household can exceed the amount used for all other purposes in the entire year. This is especially true in hot, dry climates.

---

*Households that manually water with a hose typically use 33 percent less water outdoors than those who use an automatic irrigation system.*

---

Many people believe that stunning gardens and beautiful lawns are only possible through extensive watering, fertilization, and pesticide application. However, eye-catching gardens and landscapes that save water, prevent pollution, and protect the environment are, in fact, easily achieved. . . .

## Water-Efficient Irrigation Systems and Practices

With common watering practices, a large portion of the water applied to lawns and gardens is not absorbed by the plants. It is lost through evaporation, runoff, or by watering too quickly or in excess of the plants' needs. Efficient irrigation systems and practices reduce these losses by applying only as much water as is needed to keep your plants and lawn healthy.

Although not watering your lawn, garden, or other landscape is the most water-efficient practice, sometimes irrigation is necessary. Irrigating lawns, gardens, and landscapes can be accomplished either manually or with an automatic irrigation system.

Manual watering with a hand-held hose tends to be the most water-efficient method, as households that manually water with a hose typically use 33 percent less water outdoors than those who use an automatic irrigation system. Households with automatic timers use 47 percent more water; those with in-ground sprinkler systems use 35 percent more water; and those with drip irrigation systems use 16 percent more water than households that manually water.

Drip-type irrigation systems, including water efficient spray heads, are considered the most efficient of the automated irrigation methods because they deliver water directly to the plants' roots. In-ground sprinkler and drip irrigation systems need to be operated and maintained properly to be water-efficient. Install system controllers such as rain sensors that prevent sprinklers from turning on during and immediately after rainfall, or soil moisture sensors that activate sprinklers only when soil moisture levels drop below pre-programmed levels. . . .

---

*Water in the early morning—if you water at mid-day, much of the water just evaporates.*

---

## Less Is More

Did you know that watering too much or too little is the cause of many common plant health problems? You can have healthier plants, save money on water bills, and conserve precious water resources by learning to give your lawn and garden just what they need, and no more.

If you step on your lawn and the grass springs back, it does not need to be watered. In addition to wasting water, over-watering can increase leaching of fertilizers into ground water and can harm your lawn and plants. Watering plants too much and too frequently also results in shallow roots, weed growth, disease, and fungus. Familiarize yourself with the settings on your irrigation controller and adjust the watering schedule regularly to conform with seasonal weather conditions.

Use alternative sources of water. To further reduce your water consumption, consider using alternative sources of irrigation water, such as gray water, reclaimed water, and collected rainwater via rain barrels. Most of the water we use to irrigate landscapes is treated, potable drinking water. By reducing the amount of drinking water used for landscape irrigation, we reduce the burden on water treatment facilities, which helps reduce the need for water treatment works expansion. Homes with access to alternative sources of irrigation water can reduce their water bills significantly. However, in some drought-prone localities, reclaiming water is not allowed; therefore, check with public health or municipal officials before using alternative sources of water. Information on local water regulations may be available on local government Web sites.

Make every drop count. The typical single-family suburban household uses at least 30 percent of their water for irrigation. Some experts estimate that more than 50 percent of landscape water goes to waste due to evaporation or runoff caused by over-watering.

## Water-Saving Tips

Easy ways to lower water bills and get more water to plants include:

- Water in the early morning—if you water at mid-day, much of the water just evaporates. Evening watering should be avoided because it can encourage the growth of mold or plant diseases.

- Water lawns separately from other plantings. Make sure sprinklers are not watering pavement.

- Water new trees and shrubs longer and less frequently than shallow-rooted plants, which require smaller amounts of water more often. Use soaker hoses or drip irrigation systems for trees and shrubs. Note: Once established, trees and shrubs in many areas of the U.S. generally do not require any watering, exceptions being arid regions.

- When using a hose, control the flow with an automatic shut-off nozzle.

- Minimize or eliminate chemical fertilizing, which artificially promotes new growth that will need additional watering.

- Raise your lawn mower cutting height—longer grass blades help shade each other, reduce evaporation, and inhibit weed growth.

- When soil is dry or compacted, it won't absorb water quickly. If water puddles, stop watering until the water has time to soak in.

- Amend your soil with compost and mulch to hold water and reduce evaporation.

- When outdoor use of city or well water is restricted during a drought, use the leftover water from the bath or sink on plants or the garden. Don't use water that contains bleach, automatic-dishwashing detergent, fabric softener, or other chemicals.

- In a dry spell, you can also allow an established lawn to go dormant in non-arid parts of the country. Water just once a month and brown areas of the lawn will bounce back in the fall. . . .

## Water Use and Energy

You may wonder what water use and energy have to do with each other. In most cases, electricity or gas are used to heat water, and this costs you money. In addition, your water utility uses energy to purify and pump water to your home, as well as treat sewage generated by the community. Currently, about eight percent of U.S. energy demand goes to treating, pumping, and heating water, which is enough electricity to power more than 5 million homes for an entire year. Water heating also accounts for 19 percent of home energy use.

By reducing your household water use, you not only reduce your water bill, but you also help to reduce the energy required to pump and treat public water supplies. In addition, by reducing water use and saving energy in the process, you are decreasing the amount of greenhouse gases produced to generate electricity, thereby helping to address climate change. In fact:

- If just 1 percent of American homes replaced an older toilet with a new WaterSense labeled toilet, the country would save more than 38 million kilowatt-hours of electricity—enough electricity to power more than 43,000 households for one month.

- If one out of every 100 American homes were retrofitted with water-efficient fixtures, we could save about 100 million kilowatt hours (kWh) of electricity per year—avoiding 80,000 tons of greenhouse gas emissions. That is equivalent to removing nearly 15,000 automobiles from the road for one year!

- If 20 percent of U.S. homes used high-efficiency clothes washers, national energy savings could be 285 billion BTUs per day—enough to supply the energy needs of over one million homes.

# Using Green Cleaning Products Has Health and Environmental Benefits

*Carol Ruth Weber*

*Carol Ruth Weber is a freelance writer based in Long Island, New York.*

*Using green cleaning products that are free of harsh chemicals can have a variety of benefits for consumers and the environment. Studies have shown that conventional cleaning products increase the risk that users will develop asthma, so using green products instead can improve air quality and minimize that risk. Green products are less corrosive and safer to use than conventional cleaners, and using fewer chemicals also means generating less water and air pollution. Homemade green cleaners are another option. In addition to being healthier for both humans and the environment, homemade cleaners based on vinegar and lemon juice are substantially cheaper than store-bought products.*

As lives become busier, over-scheduled and more stressful, it's easy to gravitate towards the latest products that promise to make annoying chores even easier. Need a bathroom cleaner? On your next trip to the store, you grab one of the many bright and colorful bottles promising to be a quick fix. But did you ever think about what's in that container?

Whether you're a housekeeper who cleans with these products all day or someone who cleans your own home regularly, you should take the time to consider it.

Most are made up of harsh cocktails of chemicals, which can be bad for your health—and your kids' health. As people rethink what they're bringing into their homes, they're looking for greener solutions.

---

*As concerns for health become more prevalent and people become more aware of the harsh effects cleaning chemicals are having, they're going back to basics and looking for greener ways to clean.*

---

Two experts Leslie Reichert, author of *Joy of Green Cleaning*, and Sara Snow, author of *Sara Snow's Fresh Living*, share the reasons why people should make the switch to green cleaning products.

## Green Cleaning Solutions

Want to try green cleaning for yourself? Read up on Green Cleaning: 12 Natural Solutions that Really Work:

1. *Healthier Home*

If you go green, "No longer will there be chemicals absorbed into the skin or breathed in by the person cleaning," Reichert says. Health benefits extend to family members who are no longer breathing in cleaners lingering in the air and sitting on surfaces.

Studies have shown that using a household cleaning spray, even as little as once a week, raises the risk of developing asthma. Snow says that using green cleaning products can reduce the chances of developing asthma, which "today is the most common chronic illness and the leading cause of school absences due to chronic illness across the country."

### 2. Purer Environment

When you use many cleaning products, "harmful chemicals are being released into the environment," says Reichert. Not great for you and the people around you to breathe in.

Changing to greener methods, "helps reduce pollution to our waterways and the air and it minimizes your impact on ozone depletion and global climate change with fewer smog-producing chemicals," advises Snow. Many green products also use recyclable packaging which minimizes waste.

### 3. Safer Products

Conventional cleaning products pose risks such as chemical burns to the cleaner's skin and eyes. Green cleaners aren't corrosive and meet strict standards regarding inhalation toxicity, combustibility and skin absorption.

### 4. Better Air Quality

As with most people, Snow can't stand the "stench of strong chemical odors." Many green cleaning products—including store bought and ones you can make at home—include pleasant natural essential oils. Reichert even refers to cleaning with these products as her "aromatherapy."

### 5. Less Expensive

"For home cleaning, vinegar, olive oil, lemon juice, etc. can do the trick for pennies on the dollar, compared to buying conventional cleaning products," Snow says. Why go out and buy products when you can use things you already have in your pantry?

Investing in green products also makes sense for companies. "The cost of environmentally friendly cleaning products has become much more competitive, while cleaning in an environmentally sound way reduces the risk of sick days for employees and the risk of fires and chemical spills," mentions Snow.

### 6. Fewer Antibacterials

Do you really need to look for products that say "antibacterial"? "We're now told by the U.S. Food and Drug Administration (FDA) that washing with antibacterial soaps isn't any better than regular soaps, and the American Medical Association (AMA) says that the frequent use of antibacterial ingredients can promote bacterial resistance to antibiotics," Snow says. "Triclosan, a common antibacterial agent found in many soaps, [may] mess with your hormonal system and thyroid. Most green or environmentally friendly cleaning products don't contain antibacterial agents."

7. *More Knowledge of Ingredients*

Government regulations don't require ingredients to be listed on any cleaning products. This is another reason Reichert is a strong advocate for making your own products at home, so "you know exactly what the ingredients are in your cleaning recipes."

As concerns for health become more prevalent and people become more aware of the harsh effects cleaning chemicals are having, they're going back to basics and looking for greener ways to clean. To hear our experts tell it, the benefits speak for themselves.

# 7

# Green Consumerism Confers a False Sense of Making a Difference

*Richard Wilk*

*Richard Wilk is an anthropology professor at Indiana University and a member of the American Anthropological Association's Task Force on Global Climate Change.*

*The concept of green consumption—the idea that individual consumer choices make a difference when it comes to environmental sustainability, economic justice, or similar concerns—is nothing more than a symbolic gesture that fails to adequately address the deep and complex problems of consumerism. The availability of "green" consumer goods, from fair-trade coffee to recycled toilet paper, does not offset the complex moral dilemmas imbued in such products; rather, it simply promotes more consumerism while conferring a false sense of morality and the illusion of making a difference. Such "passive activism" is only a token gesture, but perhaps green consumerism will prompt some individuals to get involved with direct action.*

Greenwashing is not just for corporations anymore—it has gone personal. Instead of feeling guilty about the huge gaps between wealthy and poor, the ways consumerism causes global warming, or how our daily pleasures cause rainforest destruction and despoil the sea, we can drink a few cups of fair-trade coffee, eat a rainforest crunch bar and instantly feel better. The consumer marketplace today offers us every kind of ethical, ecological and healthy option we can imagine, from recycled toilet paper to household wind turbines.

Goodness and moral values have been privatized in our post-Reagan-Thatcher neoliberal world. "Green" consumer goods promise the eternal lie of the huckster—that we can have our cake and eat it too, that we can change the world without sacrifice, or any more effort than smarter shopping. Because our gold ear-studs have been "ethically mined" we are absolved from thinking about why we feel we "need" to wear gold at all. We can take expensive vacations in exotic tropical lands, ignoring the poverty around us while we enjoy "sustainable" gourmet meals and an organic mud bath.

---

*What is different about eco-shopping in the contemporary world is that the problems it tries to address are so much larger and more serious than the issues faced by previous generations.*

---

Green consumption reduces all of the problems of the world into making the right shopping decisions. If the World Trade Organization is helping bring sweatshop products into our local shop, it is up to us to go find some fair-traded alternative, certified by some impoverished NGO [nongovernmental organization] and its idealistic unpaid interns. When outlaw Spanish fishermen chase down the last bluefin tuna in the Mediterranean, we are supposed to find out where the tuna in our local sushi bar came from to make sure we are not partners in crime.

## A Co-opted Marketplace

From a critical distance the entire premise that justice and sustainability can be purchased in the marketplace is patently absurd. The proliferation of new consumer choices is just as likely to increase total consumption as it is to lead to actual cuts or measureable reductions. And without the intervention of trusted intermediaries, any system of certification is likely to be co-opted by producers and marketers, to the point where it just becomes another meaningless mark on a package. Products and brands that do establish some sort of trusted position among consumers are just increasing their brand value in a way that makes them vulnerable to take-overs and buy-outs. This happened with iconic counter-cultural brands in the USA like Kashi (now Kellogg) and Ben & Jerry's ice cream, which is now a division of Unilever, though you would not know this from the company website. In a marketplace now awash in green paint, candy bars have become "granola bars" from a fictional "Nature Valley," which is actually the factory of mega-corporation General Mills.

## Consumption and Morality

This is hardly the first time that frugality and morality become fashionable in the marketplace. Non-slavery sugar was an early example of social marketing, followed by the Salvation Army's manufacture of matches made without the white phosphorus that poisoned match factory workers. At the higher end of the social scale, examples include Marie Antoinette's little farm at Versailles and Theodore Roosevelt's sojourn on a western ranch, where he toughened himself and regained his masculinity. Generations of the middle class have sent their children off to summer camps to live simply with nature, and to colleges where they experience temporary poverty, hopefully relieved after graduation. Even ancient Babylonian city-dwellers worried that opulence was spoiling their children, and by the time of the European Renaissance, a large fraction of the population was living in the enforced frugality of convents and monasteries. A hunger for authenticity, direct experience, and knowledge of origins and production have been deeply embedded in elite consumption for hundreds of years, for example in the connoisseurship of French wines and foods like truffles and caviar. Even the ancient Romans loved the "simple life" on their rural villas, at the same time that they sought the finest and rarest spices, clothing, cosmetics and wines. Nostalgia for an imagined past or a perfect landscape has driven consumption, and tinged it with a deep sense of morality for a long time, perhaps since the very first cities of the late bronze age.

---

*There is a thin and often invisible line between green actions and greenwashing.*

---

## Symbolic Changes for Substantive Problems

What is different about eco-shopping in the contemporary world is that the problems it tries to address are so much larger and more serious than the issues faced by previous generations. More people live in absolute poverty, without even the ability to feed themselves on subsistence farms, than ever before in human history. Consumers have never faced such a wide range of dangers from a witches brew of toxic chemicals, resistant diseases, and engineered organisms. And we have rapidly burned through hundreds of millions of years of sequestered carbon in the form of fossil fuels, changing the composition of the planet's atmosphere in a gargantuan uncontrolled experiment in climate regulation.

Another difference between our own consumer culture and that of our ancestors, is that now we know so much more about the way our consumption connects us to each other, to our own health and that of the planet. For the first time we can see, or even talk to the people who grow our gourmet coffee, weave our artisanal rugs, and put beads in our cornrows on a holiday beach. This marvelous network of information leaves consumers more exposed to moral fault than ever before, and makes the burden of moral behavior heavier and more perilous. Often the only choices seem to be tokenism—

making changes that are more symbolic than substantive—or cynicism grounded in the experience of falling for new trends or solutions that turn out to be misguided, co-opted, or fraudulent.

## Green Consumerism Isn't Enough

Those of us concerned with the real impacts of global consumer culture are stuck in the territory between cynicism and tokenism, trying to think more productively about the kinds of strategies that can make a symbolic and material difference. We hope that the passive activism of green (or greenish) consumption can connect with more overtly political activities, from changing local health codes to allow edible landscaping or backyard chickens, seeking further education on environmental issues, or backing green candidates in elections. Green consumerism may play a key role as a kind of "gateway drug" for people who would otherwise be disengaged from any action at all. Changing your brand of toilet paper requires no more than a minimal commitment of time and money, but it might provoke some questions about the origins and impacts of other consumer goods. Fear of bad publicity or consumer boycotts has also been a powerful force in getting the attention of manufacturers and service-providers, eliciting many levels of response to issues of sustainability. But there is a thin and often invisible line between green actions and greenwashing. Sometimes we can only tell in retrospect if actions by governments and corporations really do reach the intended goal of reducing waste, increasing efficiency and promoting public health. At what point do thin coats of green paint add up to something more substantial and self-supporting?

As the $CO_2$ measuring instruments on Mauna Kea in Hawaii edges towards 400 PPM, it is time to think about more direct actions that we can take to dramatize the dilemma of consumer culture. We need to stop using abstract terms like "growth" and "industrial output" when we talk about the causes of climate change. Voluntary actions by an enlightened few are not going to change the amount of $CO_2$, methane and soot pouring into our air. Even a carbon tax is not going to solve our problem, since the rich have shown over and over again that they are willing to pay higher prices to [enjoy] their yachts, limousines and private jets. Shock treatment through dramatic public events that bring shame on high consumers, and other direct action, has to be on the agenda.

# 8

# Demand for Eco-Friendly Products Has Led to Corporate "Greenwashing"

*Greenpeace*

*Greenpeace is an environmental activism organization that works to protect the environment worldwide. StopGreenwash.org is a Greenpeace campaign that seeks to engage companies in debate and give consumers, activists, and lawmakers the information and tools they need to confront corporate deception, look beneath the veneer of green marketing, and hold corporations accountable for the impacts of their business decisions.*

*"Greenwashing" is a term used to describe the practice of representing a company or product as being more environmentally friendly than it really is via "the cynical use of environmental themes to whitewash corporate misbehavior." Companies must stop portraying the minor steps they take on the environment as big accomplishments in their effort to woo ecologically conscious consumers. The time and money companies spend trying to make themselves appear green could be much better spent actually making a difference. The Greenpeace initiative StopGreen wash.org monitors corporate greenwashing and is working to reform advertising standards and corporate codes of conduct in order to hold corporations accountable.*

These days, green is the new black. Corporations are falling all over themselves to demonstrate to current and potential customers that they are not only ecologically conscious, but also environmentally correct.

Some businesses are genuinely committed to making the world a better, greener place. But for far too many others, environmentalism is little more than a convenient slogan. Buy our products, they say, and you will end global warming, improve air quality, and save the oceans. At best, such statements stretch the truth; at worst, they help conceal corporate behavior that is environmentally harmful by any standard.

The average citizen is finding it more and more difficult to tell the difference between those companies genuinely dedicated to making a difference and those that are using a green curtain to conceal dark motives. Consumers are constantly bombarded by corporate campaigns touting green goals, programs, and accomplishments. Even when corporations voluntarily strengthen their record on the environment, they often use multi-million dollar advertising campaigns to exaggerate these minor improvements as major achievements.

Sometimes, not even the intentions are genuine. Some companies, when forced by legislation or a court decision to improve their environmental track record, promote the resulting changes as if they had taken the step voluntarily. And at the same time that many corporations are touting their new green image (and their CEOs are giving lectures on corporate ecological ethics), their lobbyists are working night and day in Washington to gut environmental protections.

---

*We believe that corporations must play a central, essential role in helping to solve the world's environmental challenges.*

---

All this—and more—is what Greenpeace calls greenwashing—the cynical use of environmental themes to whitewash corporate misbehavior. The term was coined around 1990 when some of America's worst polluters (including DuPont, Chevron, Bechtel, the American Nuclear Society, and the Society of Plastics Industry) tried to pass themselves off as eco-friendly at a trade fair taking place in Washington, DC.

## Holding Corporations Accountable

But make no mistake: corporations were using greenwashing long before that trade fair took place, and have not hesitated to use it ever since. As the public's (and the media's) environmental awareness has grown, so too has the sophistication of corporate public relations strategies. If companies had spent as much time and money improving their core business practices as they have spent making themselves look green, they might have made a real difference.

Greenpeace wants corporations to talk the talk, but not if they are merely cynically using such rhetoric to conceal their utter failure to walk the walk. We believe that corporations must play a central, essential role in helping to solve the world's environmental challenges. We believe they can do so by ending their destructive policies and by waking up to the economic benefits of environmentally sustainable practices and products.

In that spirit, we call on companies to stop portraying baby steps on the environment as giant strides. When an oil company invests in wind or solar power, every little bit helps. But we need more than "little bits" to solve global warming, halt deforestation, prevent the destruction of the oceans, and end the proliferation of toxic chemicals. As long as half-measures are sold as full solutions, corporate actions, no matter how sincere, will be nothing more than a more sophisticated form of greenwashing.

## Stop Corporate Greenwashing Behavior

Greenpeace's StopGreenwash.org continues our thirty-five year track record of monitoring corporate malfeasance, confronting polluters, and stopping environmental crimes whenever and wherever they occur. Now, using the Internet, we will

confront deceptive Greenwashing campaigns, engage companies in debate, and give consumers and activists and lawmakers the information and tools they need to confront corporate
deception, to look beneath this green veneer and hold corporations accountable for the impacts their core business decisions and investments are having on our planet.

At the same time, we will push to reform advertising standards and corporate codes of conduct (including legislative
and litigated solutions where possible), so that we can help
bring an end to the practice of greenwashing. It is our hope
that the end result will be fewer corporations pretending to
act and more taking action, in the process making the world a
safer, greener, and ultimately better place.

# 9

# Driving an Electric Car Reduces Carbon Emissions and Fuel Costs

## Union of Concerned Scientists

*The Union of Concerned Scientists is a membership organization of citizens and scientists who work together to promote the responsible use of science to improve the world.*

*Electric vehicles are no longer just concept cars; they are widely available products that are now helping to curb global warming. Because they draw power from the US electric grid rather than using gasoline, they reduce oil consumption and produce fewer global warming emissions than even most gas/electric hybrids; those emissions are even lower when cleaner energy sources contribute to a utility's power mix. Electric vehicle owners can save up to $1,200 a year compared with operating an efficient gasoline vehicle, which translates to over $18,000 in fuel savings over the vehicle's lifetime. Electric vehicles have come of age and are good for the environment and consumers alike.*

For electric vehicles (EVs), the future is here. No longer just concept models, EVs are being featured in—and rolling out of—showrooms across the country. For example, the all-electric Nissan LEAF, powered solely by batteries, and the plug-in hybrid Chevy Volt, powered both by batteries and an internal combustion engine, debuted in 2011. Automakers are introducing many new models in 2012, including the Ford Focus Electric, Toyota Prius Plug-in Hybrid, and Mitsubishi "i," with plans for many more EVs over the next several years.

These vehicles will draw some or all of their power from the U.S. electricity grid instead of the gas pump, resulting in significant reductions in the oil consumption, global warming emissions, and fueling costs of driving. However, the global warming emissions of driving an EV depend on how the electricity is generated—given that the sources of power vary among the nation's regional electricity grids—and the cost to fuel these vehicles is dependent on local utilities' electricity rates. To compare the global warming emissions and fuel-cost savings of electric vehicles with traditional gasoline-powered vehicles, consumers need access to more localized information, which has not been readily available—until now.

---

*Driving the average gasoline vehicle costs more than $18,000 to refuel over the vehicle's lifetime, but the owner of an EV can expect to pay thousands of dollars less to power his or her vehicle.*

---

This report's analysis shows that consumers should feel confident that driving an electric vehicle yields lower global warming emissions than the average new compact gasoline-powered vehicle.

In regions covering 45 percent of the nation's population, electricity is generated with a larger share of cleaner energy resources—such as renewables and natural gas—meaning that EVs produce lower global warming emissions than even the most efficient gasoline hybrids. But in regions where coal still makes up a large percentage of the electricity grid mix, the most efficient gasoline-powered hybrid vehicles will yield lower global warming emissions than an electric vehicle. Even then, however, electric vehicles slash oil consumption in nearly all regions.

Our analysis also concludes that wherever EV owners "charge up," they can save $750 to $1,200 a year compared with operating an average new compact gasoline vehicle (27 mpg) fueled with gasoline at $3.50 per gallon. At that gasoline price, driving the average gasoline vehicle costs more than $18,000 to refuel over the vehicle's lifetime, but the owner of an EV can expect to pay thousands of dollars less to power his or her vehicle. Thus, while in this early electric vehicle market these products have higher up-front costs, knowing how much one can save by using electricity instead of gasoline is an important factor for consumers considering an EV purchase. In some areas, consumers' realization of *maximum* savings may entail a switch from their current electricity rate plan to the most advantageous one offered by their utility.

In particular, this report answers the following key questions:

*Global Warming Emissions*

Where you live, does an electric vehicle have lower global warming emissions than a gasoline hybrid?

*Fuel-Cost Savings*

How much does it cost to charge an electric vehicle in 50 major cities around the country? And how can you save the most money?

## Global Warming Emissions of Electric Vehicles

Electric vehicles have no tailpipe emissions, but the production of electricity used to charge these vehicles can result in varying levels of global warming emissions as well as the release of other pollutants. When the electricity used to power the vehicle comes from resources such as wind and solar power, EVs can operate nearly emissions-free. This potential is being demonstrated today by some individuals who are pairing rooftop solar electricity systems with their electric vehicle ownership. For most electric vehicle owners, however, their cars will be charged using electricity from their region's electricity grid.

Regional differences in the mix of fuels used to generate electricity, such as coal, natural gas, nuclear, hydro, and wind, result in significant variations in global warming emissions. In other words, not all electricity sources are created equal. For example, for each unit of electricity produced, the global warming emissions of coal-fired power plants are about twice those of natural-gas-fired power plants. Burning oil to produce electricity also is very dirty, but because it accounts for less than 1 percent of total U.S. electricity generation, oil's impact on overall emissions from that sector is limited. Renewable resources such as wind and hydro, on the other hand, emit no global warming gases at all when producing electricity. Thus a region's global warming emissions intensity (global warming emissions per unit of electricity), and therefore the global warming emissions of driving an electric vehicle there, will vary according to the region's mix of power plants.

---

*Nearly half (45 percent) of Americans live in BEST regions—where an EV has lower global warming emissions than a 50 mpg gasoline-powered vehicle.*

---

The mix of electricity sources varies not only by region; it is also changing over time as older power plants are retired and the production of clean electricity increases. These changes are due in part to state and federal policies such as air pollution standards, renewable electricity standards, and tax incentives to increase clean electricity production. By 2020, global warming emissions intensity of electricity generation is expected to have improved in some regions by as much as 30 percent over 2010. That means the global warming emissions from driving an electric vehicle purchased today will likely decrease over its lifetime.

However, consumers in the market for an EV want to know how the global warming emissions of plugging in an electric vehicle compare with those of operating a gasoline vehicle today. To provide this information, we determined the global warming emissions that result from electricity consumption in the 26 "grid regions" covering the United States, and we rated each region based on how charging an electric vehicle there compares with driving a gasoline vehicle. Each regional electricity grid represents the group of power plants that together serve as the primary source of electricity for that specific area of the country.

Our ratings provide a rule of thumb for consumers in different regions when evaluating the global warming emissions footprint of an EV powered by grid electricity, relative to a gasoline-powered vehicle.

## Key Findings

Key findings include:

- Nearly half (45 percent) of Americans live in BEST regions—where an EV has lower global warming emissions than a 50 mpg gasoline-powered vehicle, topping even the best gasoline hybrids on the market. Charging an EV in the cleanest electricity regions, which include California, New York (excluding Long Island), the Pacific Northwest, and parts of Alaska, yields global warming emissions equivalent to a gasoline-powered vehicle achieving over 70 mpg.

- Some 38 percent of Americans live in BETTER regions—where an electric vehicle has the equivalent global warming emissions of a 41 to 50 mpg gasoline vehicle, similar to the best gasoline hybrids available today. For example, charging an EV in Florida and across most of Texas yields global warming emissions equivalent to a 48 mpg gasoline vehicle; this is the fuel economy level of vehicles such as the Honda Civic Hybrid (44 mpg) and Toyota Prius Hybrid (50 mpg).

- About 17 percent of Americans live in GOOD regions—where an electric vehicle has the equivalent global warming emissions of a 31 to 40 mpg gasoline vehicle, making some gasoline hybrid vehicles a better choice with respect to global warming emissions. The Rocky Mountain grid region (covering Colorado and parts of neighboring states) has the highest emissions intensity of any regional grid in the United States, which means an EV will produce global warming emissions equivalent to a gasoline vehicle achieving about 34 mpg. Gasoline-powered cars with fuel economy at this level include the Hyundai Elantra (33 mpg) and the Ford Fiesta (34 mpg).

---

*When charging on the lowest-cost electricity plan, EV owners can save $750 to $1,200 per year in fuel costs compared with the cost of operating the average compact gasoline vehicle.*

---

## Fuel-Cost Savings of Electric Vehicles

Electric vehicles currently offered by manufacturers come with a wide range of price tags, ranging from luxury sports cars with $100,000 sticker prices to more modest four- and five-passenger vehicles, some of which can be purchased for under $30,000 (when factoring in an available $7,500 federal tax credit). While electric vehicles today cost more to purchase than comparable gasoline vehicles and, if faster charging is desired, require some up-front investment in home equipment, EV owners can realize significant fuel-cost savings compared with operating a gasoline vehicle because driving on electricity is cheaper. An EV driver could save 6,100 gallons of gasoline and nearly $13,000 over the life of the vehicle relative to today's average compact gasoline car, assuming a national average electricity price and $3.50-per-gallon gasoline. But electricity rates vary among cities and utilities across the country, and many utilities offer optional rate plans that can benefit EV owners. In the 50 most populous cities in the United States, driving on electricity will save money compared with driving the average gasoline vehicle, but taking advantage of utility rate plans that offer lower-cost electricity at night may provide additional savings of hundreds of dollars per year for EV owners.

Our analysis compiled information from utilities serving those 50 cities to determine the cost of charging an EV on different rate plans and we then evaluated how much owners could save on fuel costs. Most electric vehicles being offered by automakers today are small to midsize cars, so fuel-cost savings from EVs were compared with the average new compact gasoline vehicle, which has an EPA city/highway fuel economy rating of 27 miles per gallon.

When charging on the lowest-cost electricity plan, EV owners can save $750 to $1,200 per year in fuel costs compared with the cost of operating the average compact gasoline vehicle (27 mpg) at gasoline prices of $3.50 per gallon. This finding represents a reduction in fueling costs of 50 to 85 percent every year. In the cities with the lowest-cost electricity, such as Oklahoma City and Indianapolis, an EV owner could save more than $1,200 a year. Even in Philadelphia, which offers the most modest savings among the 50 cities evaluated, an EV owner could still save more than $750 per year in fuel costs.

Even when their electric vehicles are compared with a 50 mpg gasoline-powered vehicle, EV owners can save $100 to $570 per year in fuel costs when using the lowest-cost rate plans. This means a cutting of fuel costs by 10 to 75 percent relative to today's most fuel-efficient gasoline-powered vehicle.

Switching from a standard rate plan to a time-of-use (TOU) rate plan and then charging the car primarily when electricity is cheapest can mean hundreds of dollars in additional savings per year, especially in California cities. Time-of-use rates often offer the best EV charging costs. Thirty-nine out of the 56 utilities serving the 50 cities evaluated offer TOU rates, and all but four were estimated to save money on EV charging compared with the standard rate. In many California cities, EV owners paying TOU rates could realize savings of more than $500 per year compared with staying on standard residential rate plans.

---

*Remember that the emissions caused by a vehicle you buy today will likely decrease over its lifetime as the electricity grid (according to projections) becomes cleaner.*

---

In every one of the 50 cities, EV owners will save money on fueling costs compared with the average compact gasoline vehicle—even without changing to the lowest-rate plans. In 44 of the 50 largest cities (88 percent), the standard electricity rate plan offers savings compared with even the best gasoline hybrid (50 mpg). The only exceptions are some California cities, where a switch to time-of-use plans is necessary to top the best gasoline hybrid (assuming a gas price of $3.50 per gallon). . . .

## Consumer Advice

Electric vehicles can help enhance our nation's energy and economic security by reducing the consumption of oil and the emissions of global warming pollutants. And while costing more up front than a gasoline vehicle, EVs can save thousands of dollars on refueling costs over their lifetimes compared with those of gasoline vehicles. Purchasing an electric vehicle today can help support an early market for these technologies and send a strong signal to automakers to continue investing in them, while tax incentives from the federal and some state governments can help make EVs more affordable.

Here is some advice, based on the findings of our analysis, for consumers considering the purchase of an electric vehicle.

*Use our regional ratings to estimate global warming emissions.* To estimate the global warming emissions of an EV in your region, use the regional ratings in this analysis as a rule of thumb. For plug-in hybrid-electric vehicles, which are powered both by electricity and gasoline, these ratings apply to the portion of miles driven on electricity. We assume an EV with an efficiency of 0.34 kWh/mile, but an EV that uses less electricity per mile will have even lower emissions than our ratings imply. And remember that the emissions caused by a vehicle you buy today will likely decrease over its lifetime as the electricity grid (according to projections) becomes cleaner.

*Consider your options for buying cleaner electricity, especially in GOOD regions.* Consumer demand for renewable electricity sends a strong signal to business people and policy makers and thus can help to stimulate more investments in renewable energy projects. Increasing GOOD regions' fraction of renewable energy sources and decreasing their reliance on coal-powered electricity will help move them into the BETTER and BEST categories.

*Support clean vehicles and clean energy polices.* Support state, regional, and federal policies, such as renewable electricity standards and tax incentives, that increase the availability of renewable electricity. These policies ensure that your contribution to tackling climate change by investing in an electric vehicle will only grow more significant over time.

*Use our charging costs as an estimate, but contact your utility for more information.* If you live in one the 50 cities we evaluated for charging costs (or live nearby and are served by the same utility), use our estimates for an idea of how much you might expect to save. But be sure to contact your utility for the latest information on rate-plan options for EV charging and to obtain estimates of charging costs and any up-front costs that might be involved.

---

*As the market for EVs expands, we must phase out the highest-emitting electricity sources, such as coal, and increase the use of cleaner and renewable alternatives.*

---

*Consider switching to a time-of-use rate plan, especially in California.* TOU plans typically offer cheaper rates in the early-morning hours, so if vehicle charging is primarily overnight, as is likely for many EV owners, a TOU plan can be a good option. If your home's electricity consumption is high during the day (when TOU rates typically are high), consider your options for charging the electric vehicle on a TOU-EV rate. Consumers should ask their utility to estimate any changes in their household electricity costs as a result of switching to a TOU-WH rate and any costs associated with installing a separate meter for a TOU-EV rate.

*Remember: even on standard rate plans, EV charging is cheaper than fueling the average compact gasoline vehicle.* EV owners should get educated on what options, such as TOU plans, are available from their utility, but also keep in mind that most "plain vanilla" standard rate plans across the country will still deliver significant fuel-cost savings compared with operating the average compact gasoline vehicle.

To learn more about electric vehicle technology, visit our website at *www.ucsusa.org/model-e.*

## Clean Cars, Clean Energy—Getting from Here to There

Major automakers' introduction of electricity-powered vehicles may be an early signal of our transition toward a virtually zero-emissions and oil-free transportation future. To make this transition a success, however, the electricity grid needs to evolve alongside our vehicles. As the market for EVs expands, we must phase out the highest-emitting electricity sources, such as coal, and increase the use of cleaner and renewable alternatives. Only by taking both types of actions in parallel—increasing the numbers of electric vehicles while cleaning up our electricity grid—can EVs fulfill their potential.

Making electric vehicles an affordable choice for greater numbers of consumers is also important to ensuring continued progress away from gasoline-powered cars and trucks. Electricity-purchasing options that offer low rates to encourage off-peak charging at certain times of the day can help EV buyers save money while also allowing utilities and electricity grid operators to better manage that grid. Utilities and regulators can help increase consumer access to low vehicle-charging rates in two important ways: by making TOU plans available to more people in more cities, and by making it easier to separate EV charging from home electricity consumption.

Driving on clean electricity promises to play a major role both in ending the United States' oil addiction and in slowing global climate change. But because the transition from oil will take time, investments in clean energy and advanced vehicle technologies must be sustained. The good news is that electric vehicles are off to a running start.

# 10

# Biofuels Are Not a Green Alternative to Fossil Fuels

*Andrew Steer and Craig Hanson*

*Andrew Steer is president of the World Resources Institute (WRI), an independent, nonprofit, and nonpartisan global research organization that works to create equity and prosperity through sustainable natural resource management. Craig Hanson is WRI's global director of food, forest, and water programs.*

*Although biofuels, such as biodiesel or ethanol made from corn, seem like a good way to reduce dependence on fossil fuels and help reduce global warming, it is not a good idea to dedicate land to cultivating them for several reasons. First and foremost, the demand for biofuel crops increases competition for land that is needed for food production, a concern that will grow more serious as the global population increases in the coming decades. Growing biofuel crops is an inefficient use of land, and biofuels do not even cut greenhouse gases as intended because burning biomass emits carbon dioxide just like fossil fuels do.*

Powering cars with corn and burning wood to make electricity might seem like a way to lessen dependence on fossil fuels and help solve the climate crisis. But although some forms of bioenergy can play a helpful role, dedicating land specifically for generating bioenergy is unwise. It uses land needed for food production and carbon storage, it requires large areas to generate just a small amount of fuel, and it won't typically cut greenhouse gas emissions.

First, dedicating areas to bioenergy production increases competition for land.

Roughly three-quarters of the world's vegetated land is already being used to meet people's need for food and forest products, and that demand is expected to rise by 70% or more by 2050. Much of the rest contains natural ecosystems that keep climate-warming carbon out of the atmosphere, protect freshwater supplies, and preserve biodiversity.

Because land and the plants growing on it are already generating these benefits, diverting land—even degraded, under-utilised areas—to bioenergy means sacrificing much-needed food, timber, and carbon storage.

---

*Bioenergy that makes dedicated use of land does not generally cut greenhouse gas emissions.*

---

Second, bioenergy production is an inefficient use of land.

While photosynthesis may do a great job of converting the sun's rays into food, it is an inefficient way to turn solar radiation into non-food energy that people can use. Thus, it takes a lot of land (and water) to yield a small amount of fuel from plants. In a new working paper, World Resources Institute (WRI) calculates that providing just 10% of the world's liquid transportation fuel in the year 2050 would require nearly 30% of all the energy in a year's worth of crops the world produces today.

## Massive Biomass Demands

The push for bioenergy extends beyond transportation fuels to the harvest of trees and other sources of biomass for electricity and heat generation. Some research suggests that bioenergy could meet 20% of the world's total annual energy demand by 2050. Yet doing so would require an amount of plants equal to all the world's current crop harvests, plant residues, timber, and grass consumed by livestock—a true non-starter.

Third, bioenergy that makes dedicated use of land does not generally cut greenhouse gas emissions.

Burning biomass, whether directly as wood or in the form of ethanol or biodiesel, emits carbon dioxide just like burning fossil fuels. In fact, burning biomass directly emits a bit more carbon dioxide than fossil fuels for the same amount of generated energy. But most calculations claiming that bioenergy reduces greenhouse gas emissions relative to burning fossil fuels do not include the carbon dioxide released when biomass is burned. They exclude it based on the assumption that this release of carbon dioxide is matched and implicitly offset by the carbon dioxide absorbed by the plants growing the biomass.

## Diversion to Bioenergy Is Bad

Yet if those plants were going to grow anyway, simply diverting them to bioenergy does not remove any additional carbon from the atmosphere and therefore does not offset the emissions from burning that biomass. Furthermore, when natural forests are felled to generate bioenergy or to replace the farm fields that were diverted to growing biofuels, greenhouse gas emissions go up.

---

*Using crops or land for biofuels competes with food production, making this goal [of feeding the world's population] even more difficult.*

---

That said, some forms of bioenergy do not increase competition with food or land, and using them instead of fossil fuels could reduce greenhouse gas emissions. One example is biomass grown in excess of what would have grown without the demand for bioenergy, such as winter cover crops for energy. Others include timber processing wastes, urban waste wood, landfill methane, and modest amounts of agriculture residues.

Using so-called second-generation technologies to convert material such as crop residues into bioenergy has a role to play and avoids competition for land. A challenge will be to do this at scale, since most of these residues are already used for animal feed or needed for soil fertility, and others are expensive to harvest.

## What Are the Alternatives?

There are good alternatives to bioenergy made from dedicated land. For example, solar photovoltaic (PV) cells convert sunlight directly into energy that people can use, much like bioenergy, but with greater efficiency and less water use. On three-quarters of the world's land, solar PV systems today can generate more than 100 times the usable energy per hectare as bioenergy. Because electric motors can be two to three times more efficient than internal combustion engines, solar PV can result in 200 to 300 times as much usable energy per hectare for vehicle transport compared to bioenergy.

One of the great challenges of our generation is how the world can sustainably feed a population expected to reach 9.6 billion by 2050. Using crops or land for biofuels competes with food production, making this goal even more difficult.

The world's land is a finite resource. As Earth becomes more crowded, fertile land and the plants it supports become ever more valuable for food, timber and carbon storage—things for which we don't have an alternative source.

# 11

# Renewable Energy Sources Benefit Health, Climate, and the Economy

*Union of Concerned Scientists*

*The Union of Concerned Scientists is a membership organization of citizens and scientists who work together to promote the responsible use of science to improve the world.*

*Renewable energy sources, such as solar, wind, geothermal, hydroelectric, and biomass, each come with their own set of unique costs and benefits, but overall these cleaner energy sources have overwhelmingly positive effects on the climate, human health, and the economy. Renewable energy sources represent a vast and inexhaustible supply of energy, produce little or no global warming emissions, improve public health and environmental quality, help stabilize energy prices, create jobs and other economic benefits, and contribute to a more reliable and resilient energy system. The costs of renewable energy have declined in recent years and are projected to continue decreasing, making renewables more accessible and affordable for consumers than ever.*

Renewable energy—wind, solar, geothermal, hydroelectric, and biomass—provides substantial benefits for our climate, our health, and our economy:

Each source of renewable energy has unique benefits and costs; this page explores the many benefits associated with these energy technologies. . . .

Human activity is overloading our atmosphere with carbon dioxide and other global warming emissions, which trap heat, steadily drive up the planet's temperature, and create significant and harmful impacts on our health, our environment, and our climate.

Electricity production accounts for more than one-third of U.S. global warming emissions, with the majority generated by coal-fired power plants, which produce approximately 25 percent of total U.S. global warming emissions; natural gas-fired power plants produce 6 percent of total emissions. In contrast, most renewable energy sources produce little to no global warming emissions.

## A Look at the Numbers

According to data aggregated by the International Panel on Climate Change, life-cycle global warming emissions associated with renewable energy—including manufacturing, installation, operation and maintenance, and dismantling and decommissioning—are minimal.

---

*Generating electricity from renewable energy rather than fossil fuels offers significant public health benefits.*

---

Compared with natural gas, which emits between 0.6 and 2 pounds of carbon dioxide equivalent per kilowatt-hour ($CO_2E$/kWh), and coal, which emits between 1.4 and 3.6 pounds of $CO_2E$/kWh, wind emits only 0.02 to 0.04 pounds of $CO_2E$/kWh, solar 0.07 to 0.2, geothermal 0.1 to 0.2, and hydroelectric between 0.1 and 0.5. Renewable electricity generation from biomass can have a wide range of global warming emissions depending on the resource and how it is harvested. Sustainably sourced biomass has a low emissions footprint, while unsustainable sources of biomass can generate significant global warming emissions.

Increasing the supply of renewable energy would allow us to replace carbon-intensive energy sources and significantly reduce U.S. global warming emissions. For example, a 2009 UCS analysis found that a 25 percent by 2025 national renewable electricity standard would lower power plant $CO_2$ emissions 277 million metric tons annually by 2025—the equivalent of the annual output from 70 typical (600 MW) new coal plants. In addition, a ground-breaking study by the U.S. Department of Energy's National Renewable Energy Laboratory explored the feasibility and environmental impacts associated with generating 80 percent of the country's electricity from renewable sources by 2050 and found that global warming emissions from electricity production could be reduced by approximately 81 percent.

## Improved Public Health and Environmental Quality

Generating electricity from renewable energy rather than fossil fuels offers significant public health benefits. The air and water pollution emitted by coal and natural gas plants is linked to breathing problems, neurological damage, heart attacks, and cancer. Replacing fossil fuels with renewable energy has been found to reduce premature mortality and lost workdays, and it reduces overall healthcare costs. The aggregate national economic impact associated with these health impacts of fossil fuels is between $361.7 and $886.5 billion, or between 2.5 percent and 6 percent of gross domestic product (GDP).

Wind, solar, and hydroelectric systems generate electricity with no associated air pollution emissions. While geothermal and biomass energy systems emit some air pollutants, total air emissions are generally much lower than those of coal- and natural gas-fired power plants.

In addition, wind and solar energy require essentially no water to operate and thus do not pollute water resources or strain supply by competing with agriculture, drinking water systems, or other important water needs. In contrast, fossil fuels can have a significant impact on water resources. For example, both coal mining and natural gas drilling can pollute sources of drinking water. Natural gas extraction by hydraulic fracturing (fracking) requires large amounts of water and all thermal power plants, including those powered by coal, gas, and oil, withdraw and consume water for cooling.

---

*Numerous studies have repeatedly shown that renewable energy can be rapidly deployed to provide a significant share of future electricity needs, even after accounting for potential constraints.*

---

Biomass and geothermal power plants, like coal- and natural gas-fired power plants, require water for cooling. In addition, hydroelectric power plants impact river ecosystems both upstream and downstream from the dam. However, NREL's 80 percent by 2050 renewable energy study, which included biomass and geothermal, found that water withdrawals would decrease 51 percent to 58 percent by 2050 and water consumption would be reduced by 47 percent to 55 percent.

## A Vast and Inexhaustible Energy Supply

Throughout the United States, strong winds, sunny skies, plant residues, heat from the earth, and fast-moving water can each provide a vast and constantly replenished energy resource supply. These diverse sources of renewable energy have the technical potential to provide all the electricity the nation needs many times over.

Estimates of the technical potential of each renewable energy source are based on their overall availability given certain technological and environmental constraints. In 2012, NREL found that together, renewable energy sources have the technical potential to supply 482,247 billion kilowatt-hours of electricity annually. This amount is 118 times the amount of electricity the nation currently consumes. However, it is important to note that not all of this technical potential can be tapped due to conflicting land use needs, the higher short-term costs of those resources, constraints on ramping up their use such as limits on transmission capacity, barriers to public acceptance, and other hurdles.

Today, renewable energy provides only a tiny fraction of its potential electricity output in the United States and worldwide. But numerous studies have repeatedly shown that renewable energy can be rapidly deployed to provide a significant share of future electricity needs, even after accounting for potential constraints.

## Jobs and Other Economic Benefits

Compared with fossil fuel technologies, which are typically mechanized and capital intensive, the renewable energy industry is more labor-intensive. This means that, on average, more jobs are created for each unit of electricity generated from renewable sources than from fossil fuels.

Renewable energy already supports thousands of jobs in the United States. For example, in 2011, the wind energy industry directly employed 75,000 full-time-equivalent employees in a variety of capacities, including manufacturing, project development, construction and turbine installation, operations and maintenance, transportation and logistics, and financial, legal, and consulting services. More than 500 factories in the United States manufacture parts for wind turbines, and the amount of domestically manufactured equipment used in wind turbines has grown dramatically in recent years: from 35 percent in 2006 to 70 percent in 2011.

Other renewable energy technologies employ even more workers. In 2011, the solar industry employed approximately 100,000 people on a part-time or full-time basis, including jobs in solar installation, manufacturing, and sales; the hydroelectric power industry employed approximately 250,000 people in 2009; and in 2010 the geothermal industry employed 5,200 people.

---

*In addition to creating new jobs, increasing our use of renewable energy offers other important economic development benefits.*

---

Increasing renewable energy has the potential to create still more jobs. In 2009, the Union of Concerned Scientists conducted an analysis of the economic benefits of a 25 percent renewable energy standard by 2025; it found that such a policy would create more than three times as many jobs as producing an equivalent amount of electricity from fossil fuels—resulting in a benefit of 202,000 new jobs in 2025.

In addition to the jobs directly created in the renewable energy industry, growth in renewable energy industry creates positive economic "ripple" effects. For example, industries in the renewable energy supply chain will benefit, and unrelated local businesses will benefit from increased household and business incomes.

## Good for the Economy

In addition to creating new jobs, increasing our use of renewable energy offers other important economic development benefits. Local governments collect property and income taxes and other payments from renewable energy project owners. These revenues can help support vital public services, especially in rural communities where projects are often located. Owners of the land on which wind projects are built also often receive lease payments ranging from $3,000 to $6,000 per megawatt of installed capacity, as well as payments for power line easements and road rights-of-way. Or they may earn royalties based on the project's annual revenues. Similarly, farmers and rural landowners can generate new sources of supplemental income by producing feedstocks for biomass power facilities.

UCS analysis found that a 25 by 2025 national renewable electricity standard would stimulate $263.4 billion in new capital investment for renewable energy technologies, $13.5 billion in new landowner income biomass production and/or wind land lease payments, and $11.5 billion in new property tax revenue for local communities.

Renewable energy projects therefore keep money circulating within the local economy, and in most states renewable electricity production would reduce the need to spend money on importing coal and natural gas from other places. Thirty-eight states were net importers of coal in 2008—from other states and, increasingly, other countries: 16 states spent a total of more than $1.8 billion on coal from as far away as Colombia, Venezuela, and Indonesia, and 11 states spent more than $1 billion each on net coal imports.

## Stable Energy Prices

Renewable energy is providing affordable electricity across the country right now, and can help stabilize energy prices in the future.

The costs of renewable energy technologies have declined steadily, and are projected to drop even more. For example, the average price of a solar panel has dropped almost 60 percent since 2011. The cost of generating electricity from wind dropped more than 20 percent between 2010 and 2012 and more than 80 percent since 1980. In areas with strong wind resources like Texas, wind power can compete directly with fossil fuels on costs. The cost of renewable energy will decline even further as markets mature and companies increasingly take advantage of economies of scale.

While renewable facilities require upfront investments to build, once built they operate at very low cost and, for most technologies, the fuel is free. As a result, renewable energy prices are relatively stable over time. UCS's analysis of the economic benefits of a 25 percent renewable electricity standard found that such a policy would lead to 4.1 percent lower natural gas prices and 7.6 percent lower electricity prices by 2030.

---

*Long-term renewable energy investments can help utilities save money they would otherwise spend to protect their customers from the volatility of fossil fuel prices.*

---

In contrast, fossil fuel prices can vary dramatically and are prone to substantial price swings. For example, there was a rapid increase in U.S. coal prices due to rising global demand before 2008, then a rapid fall after 2008 when global demands declined. Likewise, natural gas prices have fluctuated greatly since 2000.

Using more renewable energy can lower the prices of and demand for natural gas and coal by increasing competition and diversifying our energy supplies. An increased reliance on renewable energy can help protect consumers when fossil fuel prices spike.

In addition, utilities spend millions of dollars on financial instruments to hedge themselves from these fossil fuel price uncertainties. Since hedging costs are not necessary for electricity generated from renewable sources, long-term renewable energy investments can help utilities save money they would otherwise spend to protect their customers from the volatility of fossil fuel prices.

# A More Reliable and Resilient Energy System

Wind and solar are less prone to large-scale failure because they are distributed and modular. Distributed systems are spread out over a large geographical area, so a severe weather event in one location will not cut off power to an entire region. Modular systems are composed of numerous individual wind turbines or solar arrays. Even if some of the equipment in the system is damaged, the rest can typically continue to operate.

For example, in 2012 Hurricane Sandy damaged fossil fuel-dominated electric generation and distribution systems in New York and New Jersey and left millions of people without power. In contrast, renewable energy projects in the Northeast weathered Hurricane Sandy with minimal damage or disruption.

The risk of disruptive events will also increase in the future as droughts, heat waves, more intense storms, and increasingly severe wildfires become more frequent due to global warming. Renewable energy sources are more resilient than coal, natural gas, and nuclear power plants in the face of these sorts of extreme weather events.

For example, coal, natural gas, and nuclear power depend on large amounts of water for cooling, and limited water availability during a severe drought or heat wave puts electricity generation at risk. Wind and solar photovoltaic systems do not require water to generate electricity, and they can help mitigate risks associated with water scarcity.

# 12

# Renewable Energy Sources Make the Power Grid More Difficult to Manage

*Kim Smuga-Otto*

*Kim Smuga-Otto is a staff writer for the* San Jose Mercury News, *a daily newspaper in the San Francisco Bay Area.*

*Renewable energy sources—such as solar, wind, geothermal, and hydroelectric—make up an increasingly large portion of the power supply in many states, but their inclusion in the power mix can cause headaches for power grid operators who must meet fluctuating consumer demand. That's because, for example, the peak time for producing solar energy (daytime) does not correspond to the peak time of consumer power use (evening), and there is nowhere to store the excess energy in the meantime. Conversely, when there is a dip in available energy, most power plants are not able to ramp up quickly enough to make up for it. Since nearly a quarter of its electricity now comes from renewable sources, California is leading the pack in navigating such power grid management issues.*

California's electrical grid has a problem—a nice problem, but a problem nonetheless: The state often has too much power.

Nearly 23 percent of California's energy now comes from renewable sources such as wind and solar, and the state is on track to reach its goal of generating one-third of its energy from renewables by 2020. But feeding all that green energy into the Golden State's grid—without overloading it—has become a major challenge.

That's because the state's aging natural gas plants aren't nimble enough to turn off when the sun starts shining and then quickly switch back on when it gets dark. And while the technology to generate clean energy is growing by leaps and bounds, efforts to store the power haven't kept up.

The dilemma has forced the energy industry to rethink the way we make and use electricity. And utilities are having to recalculate how much they should charge for electricity at certain times of the day.

---

*The last time Californians had to think about their electrical grid was in the early 2000s, when companies such as Enron manipulated energy prices and caused statewide brownouts.*

---

"I've seen more changes in the past three years than the previous 20," said Eric Schmitt, vice president of operations for the California Independent System Operator [ISO], the "air traffic control" center of one of the world's largest electrical grids. The center is capable of directing more than 50,000 megawatts of electricity—the output of almost 300 average-sized power plants running at full capacity—over high-voltage lines that crisscross the state.

## The Command Center

The ISO's home in Folsom looks like a starship's control room in a science fiction movie: 12 horseshoe-shaped tables, each with eight wide screens. A bank of colorful monitors stretches for 80 feet across one wall, flashing graphs, maps and constantly updating reports.

The last time Californians had to think about their electrical grid was in the early 2000s, when companies such as Enron manipulated energy prices and caused statewide brownouts. Since then, the nonprofit organization that oversees electricity delivery to 80 percent of the state has faded from view.

Since the late '90s, public utilities such as Pacific Gas and Electric have largely gotten out of the business of running power plants. They now buy most of the electricity their customers use from the wholesale energy market.

Roughly 140 companies sell to the market, resulting in about 27,000 transactions per day. The ISO makes sure the purchased electricity makes it to the utilities' substations.

## Duck Curves and Quick Starts

To help explain how the increases in renewable energy affect the amount of electricity available, grid operators have produced a graph they've nicknamed the Duck Curve because of its tail-belly-neck shape. The lines track California's demand for electricity over a single day, subtracting out the electricity supplied by solar and wind.

In the morning, electricity demand rises as people wake up and turn on appliances, lights and electric toothbrushes. And as the day wears on, the state is increasingly dependent on solar plants, especially in the afternoon.

A recent record was set on March 6 [2015], when solar peaked at 5,812 megawatts, five times what it was three years ago. All this solar power is allowing California to cut back on natural gas—which now provides about 60 percent of the state's energy needs—and other traditional sources of electricity.

But this can be a problem because the sun sets at the same time that people are returning home. That causes electricity use to surge, and the power plants that were turned down or even off need to start producing—fast.

The majority of California's power plants, however, aren't up for the abrupt on-and-off challenge. "A big portion of our fleet is not flexible," said Steven Greenlee, an ISO spokesman. "It cannot be ramped up fast. It cannot start and stop multiple times."

---

*[A] quick source of electricity could come from storage— basically big batteries that would discharge to the grid when needed.*

---

It can take up to a day for a typical electrical generator to go from "off" to being able to add electricity to the grid. And as more solar comes online, the ramp-up curve each evening is getting steeper.

Greenlee said the grid needs natural gas plants that can respond to increased demand within 10 minutes. This could mean building new plants or retrofitting old ones.

## Storage Capacity

Another quick source of electricity could come from storage—basically big batteries that would discharge to the grid when needed. The storage capacity isn't there now, but the California Public Utilities Commission has mandated that PG&E, Southern California Edison and San Diego Gas and Electric have a combined 1,325 megawatts of storage no later than 2024.

Todd Strauss, PG&E's senior director of energy policy, said there are "lots of engineering challenges behind the curtain," but that the utility is on track to add its 500-megawatt share of storage on schedule.

PG&E is also looking to shift the times of its highest-priced electricity to match when demand is actually the greatest.

The utility now charges its highest rates on weekdays from 1 p.m. to 7 p.m. in the summer. But that's when the sun is supplying a great deal of energy. So the utility has petitioned the PUC to set the time back, from 4 p.m. to 9 p.m., to encourage PG&E customers to delay washing dishes or doing laundry until the demand for energy drops.

While the energy ramp-up may look like the most intimidating problem, a more immediate one is too much electricity on the grid.

Four times last year, the winds—which usually drop off in the early morning—kept blowing. Grid operators had to order a decrease of 1,700 megawatts of energy or risk damaging power lines.

"We have to take immediate action whenever the grid goes out of balance," Greenlee said. "We can't just wait and see."

Nancy Rader, executive director of the California Wind Energy Association, says that wind generation is usually a balancing force on the grid because it normally gets windier as the sun is setting. "It's going in the right direction at the right time," said Rader, who doesn't see over-generation of wind energy as much of a problem because it's easy to turn off a wind turbine.

And Joe Desmond, senior vice president of marketing for BrightSource, predicts that solar-energy generation will ultimately prove to be more flexible. The Oakland-based company that built Ivanpah in the Mojave Desert—California's largest solar plant—is designing plants for China that can store solar heat and save it for after dark.

Schmitt is also optimistic. The grid operators, he said, are up to the challenge.

"In California, we're out in front, setting the pace," he said. "We're showing folks how to do this."

# 13

# Green Building Standards Create Jobs and Save Taxpayers Money

*US Green Building Council*

*The US Green Building Council (USGBC) is a diverse group of businesses, activists, nonprofits, and lawmakers that share a vision of a sustainable built environment. Toward that end, the group established Leadership in Energy and Environmental Design (LEED), a certification program that guides the design, construction, operations, and maintenance of buildings, homes, and communities so they are environmentally responsible and use resources efficiently. LEED is the most widely used green building program in the world, certifying 1.5 million square feet of building space each day in 135 countries.*

*When governments choose to build green, LEED-certified buildings, it means more than just reducing environmental impacts and demonstrating strong environmental stewardship; it also means exercising fiscally sound governance that supports local investment, creates jobs, and saves taxpayers money for years to come through reduced water and energy consumption. Thus, green building is something that governments at all levels can be proud of getting behind.*

Government at all levels has a responsibility to use taxpayer dollars both wisely and transparently. Through its investments, governments can protect and expand the Ameri-

US Green Building Council, "LEED Saving Taxpayers Money, Creating American Jobs and Leading by Example," usgbc.org, June 2014.

can workforce and also catalyze future competitiveness and growth of domestic enterprise. High performance, LEED-certified buildings have a strong track record of serving these important goals and more. By using LEED, a voluntary, market-driven green building certification program, thousands of public buildings have saved money, demonstrated strong environmental stewardship, supported local investment, and helped create jobs. These buildings become iconic civic structures, reflecting smart, responsible and fiscally sound governance.

Just as in the private sector, new and upgraded LEED public buildings can save money by using less energy and water and by creating an environment for more productive occupants. Governments across the nation are choosing to achieve LEED certification in their public buildings to deliver the proven economic and environmental benefits of green building. For example, U.S. General Services Administration (GSA) LEED-certified government buildings use 27 percent less energy and cost 19 percent less to operate compared to the national average. GSA is a participant in the LEED Volume program, which can reduce certification fees by up to 80%.

## Accountability Makes a Difference

The U.S. Department of the Treasury's iconic headquarters, earned LEED Gold in 2011. The building, which made significant building operation improvements to slash energy and water consumption, saves taxpayers $3.5 million per year. This is just one LEED-certified federal project. Across 15 agencies and departments, the federal government has certified more than 1,500 LEED projects, driving tremendous taxpayer savings while also creating jobs and reducing environmental impacts.

For better buildings, accountability makes a difference. Through a carefully managed, independent, third-party verification system, LEED affirms the integrity of green building commitments by ensuring project teams are delivering on design plans and goals. Third-party validation helps guarantee that each project saves energy, water and other resources, reducing the overall environmental impact. No cutting corners. Taxpayers deserve to know they're getting a strong return on their investment.

---

*When governments commit to build green—and especially to LEED—it is a statement of leadership and pride.*

---

The value of green building has seen major growth from $10 billion in 2005, to an estimated $200+ billion by 2016 (nonresidential and residential). 55 percent of all commercial and institutional construction will be green by 2016, according to a recent McGraw-Hill Construction study. Such an increase translated to a massive amount of design, construction, operation and other jobs, all connected to the market-driven growth of the green building industry.

## Economic Benefits

Government is helping turn the gears of job creation while also encouraging the spread of 21$^{st}$ Century building science and technology. A Harvard Business School study found that public investment in LEED-certified government buildings stimulates private investment, supply and market uptake of greener building practice. The research finds that green public building commitments produce a near doubling effect in private investment across the building sector and up and down the supply chain of products, professionals and services—not to mention the energy and water savings. Neighboring communities experience a 60% increase in the same, all of which is encouraged by government leadership by example.

Our buildings are at the heart of our communities. Iconic buildings and city skylines become shining symbols for a city's identity. From our town halls to courthouses, from capital domes to train stations, buildings help define the places we live and work. When governments commit to build green—and especially to LEED—it is a statement of leadership and pride. Green public buildings demonstrate a commitment to a safe, stronger, and more comfortable today, without compromising a brighter, healthier, more prosperous tomorrow.

# 14

# US Green Building Standards Are Being Adopted Worldwide

*Institute for Building Efficiency*

*The Institute for Building Efficiency is a project of Johnson Controls, Inc., an American multinational corporation that offers products and services to optimize the energy and operational efficiencies of buildings, among its other business ventures.*

*The green building certification process known as Leadership in Energy and Environmental Design (LEED) has transformed building practices and become the industry standard in the United States, and its impact continues to grow as LEED standards are being adopted by builders around the world. Asia, China, Brazil, and the Middle East are some of the biggest regions that are shifting to green building practices, and more than 40 percent of total LEED-certified square footage is currently outside the United States, in more than 135 countries. The future for LEED will be as bright as its past, as new versions of the certification standard enhance the strong foundation already put in place.*

Thousands will gather in San Francisco for the annual Greenbuild International Conference and Expo, sponsored by the U.S. Green Building Council (USGBC). Industry leaders and practitioners from around the world have attended for over the past decade to learn about green building best prac-

Institute for Building Efficiency, "Reshaping Building Practices: A Look Back After a Decade of Greenbuild," November 2014, institutebe.com. Copyright © 2014 Johnson Controls. All rights reserved. Reproduced with permission.

tices and Leadership in Energy and Environmental Design (LEED®) standards, while engaging in conversations that help broaden the market for green buildings.

LEED is a voluntary, consensus-based process that rates new or existing buildings on numerous green aspects that aim to enhance sustainability, protect the environment, and promote human health. Now with nine rating systems encompassing several building and market types and spanning the entire lifecycle of buildings, the LEED rating system has paved the way for global transformation in the building industry.

## Transformative Practices Take Root

In 2002, the year of the first Greenbuild conference, there were fewer than 100 commercial LEED-certified projects; now there are more than 10,000 LEED-certified commercial buildings, and the number is growing. In the 2012 Energy Efficiency Indicator (EEI) survey from the Johnson Controls Institute for Building Efficiency, 43 percent of respondents said their organizations planned to pursue voluntary green building certifications for existing buildings in the next year, with 44 percent planning certification for new construction. Nearly 60 percent of 2012 EEI survey respondents indicated that they had at least one certified green building, up from 7 percent in 2008.

*Currently, more than 40 percent of the total LEED-registered square footage is outside the United States, in more than 135 countries.*

LEED has transformed real estate conventions around sustainable practice, and its impact continues to grow around the world. In the United States, LEED has become the new industry norm: more than 384 cities and towns, 34 state governments, 14 federal agencies and departments, and many educational institutions reference or use the LEED ratings in their green building policies.

Scot Horst, senior vice president of LEED at the USGBC, describes LEED as a leadership system to increasingly improve the performance of buildings while decreasing their environmental impact. Horst explains that LEED drove many building technology and supply companies to change the products or services they offer and that LEED became the new "due diligence" in the market. Kim Hosken, Director of Green Buildings at Johnson Controls and a LEED practitioner since its inception in 2000, noted that LEED's influence was not in products alone; it also drove education and collaborative building practices. Because of the increased education on green building practices, she explains, LEED is a quality control and improvement tool, demonstrating to building owners and operators how to further advance the status of buildings' sustainability and efficiency.

## The Globalization of Green Buildings

A most impressive and somewhat unexpected trend, according to Horst, is the adoption of the LEED rating system internationally. According the USGBC, the largest growth in LEED registrations is in Asia, and the council sees especially accelerated growth in Brazil, China and the Middle East. Currently, more than 40 percent of the total LEED-registered square footage is outside the United States, in more than 135 countries. Horst attributes this to LEED's strong global recognition and respect as a tool to promote not only sustainability, but excellence in building design, construction, operation and maintenance. In Shanghai for example, LEED is seen as a means of quality control and risk mitigation, and the market has realized the benefits of integrated design approaches through the LEED process, he observes.

The need to recognize local markets and conditions while maintaining global standards has been a discussion point for many green building market participants. In March, 2012, the USGBC and the World Green Building Council announced that points for several Energy & Atmosphere credits would be awarded in LEED for meeting criteria in BREEAM, the United Kingdom's green building rating system. This is an important step toward making LEED flexible and complementary to other global rating systems.

USGBC has also implemented Alternative Compliance Paths for several of the credits. The Alternative Compliance Paths take regionally unique issues such as weather, transportation systems and local codes into account to approach challenges in applying LEED credits around the world, while maintaining the overall credit structure and rating system consistency. For example, projects outside the U.S. may use a local benchmark based on source energy from their country's national or regional energy agency.

> *The LEED rating system has been an impetus for change, propelling the industry forward and profoundly changing the way buildings are designed, constructed, operated and maintained.*

## Where Will LEED Lead?

LEED v4 is the next stage in the LEED evolution toward global applicability and technical rigor, bringing about changes that align to international standards, recognize local issues and solutions, and foster relevance to additional markets and building types. According to Horst, performance is key in existing buildings, and the USGBC will focus on leveraging tools and systems to measure performance in order to track progress and assess success. Changes in LEED v4 are designed to promote:

- More holistic practices, such as building commissioning and the integrative design process.

• Increased emphasis on measurement and performance.

The USGBC Building Performance Initiative was announced in 2009, creating a means to track the performance of building operations and how the occupants use the space within previously LEED-certified buildings. LEED v4 will build on that work to ensure an effective structure to collect, track and report building data and enable continued improvement after certification.

Changes in the LEED rating system, most recently with LEED v4, have not come without resistance from the building industry and LEED practitioners. Horst explains that the challenge is striking a balance between keeping the LEED system the same—potentially less stringent but with wider market impact—while maintaining LEED's role to continuously push the market and foster change and improvement in the green building space.

Over the past 10 years since the first Greenbuild conference, much has changed in the building industry. The LEED rating system has been an impetus for change, propelling the industry forward and profoundly changing the way buildings are designed, constructed, operated and maintained. As the industry looks to the future, there is still much to improve and many barriers to break down, but the USGBC will continue to use LEED as a tool to push market expectations by building on the transformative framework it has established thus far.

# Organizations to Contact

*The editors have compiled the following list of organizations concerned with the issues debated in this book. The descriptions are derived from materials provided by the organizations. All have publications or information available for interested readers. The list was compiled on the date of publication of the present volume; the information provided here may change. Be aware that many organizations take several weeks or longer to respond to inquiries, so allow as much time as possible.*

**BioCycle**
63 S 7th St., Suite 5, Emmaus, PA    18049
(610) 967-4135
website: www.biocycle.net

BioCycle is recognized worldwide for its authoritative coverage on composting, organics recycling, landfill diversion, biofuels, emissions controls and renewable energy, community sustainability, urban agriculture, and green jobs and businesses. The organization hosts annual conferences and has published *BioCycle* magazine since 1960. The BioCycle.net website offers extensive information about a wide variety of green practices, product reviews, links to other green resources, and a weekly e-bulletin.

**Greenpeace/Stopgreenwash.org**
702 H St. NW, Suite 300, Washington, DC    20001
(202) 462-1177 • fax: (202) 462-4507
e-mail: info@wdc.greenpeace.org
website: www.stopgreenwash.org

Greenpeace is an environmental activism organization that works to protect the environment worldwide. The group's priorities include combating climate change, deforestation, and ocean pollution. Stopgreenwash.org is a Greenpeace campaign that seeks to engage companies in debate and give consumers, activists, and lawmakers the information and tools they need to confront corporate deception, look beneath the veneer of green marketing, and hold corporations accountable for the impacts of their business decisions. The Stopgreenwash.org website features a wide variety of reports, fact sheets, and news updates about greenwashing, as well as information about Greenpeace programs and activities.

## Institute of Scrap Recycling Industries (ISRI)

1615 L St. NW, Suite 600, Washington, DC   20036-5610
(202) 662-8500 • fax: (202) 626-0900
e-mail: isri@isri.org
website: www.isri.org

The Institute of Scrap Recycling Industries (ISRI) is the voice of the scrap recycling industry, an association of more than 1,350 companies that process, broker, and consume scrap commodities. Based in Washington, DC, the group encourages manufacturers to build electronics with safer, more easily recyclable materials and educates the public about the benefits of scrap recycling. ISRI publishes a bimonthly magazine, *Scrap*, and maintains a collection of reports, letters, and position papers on its website.

## Keep America Beautiful

1010 Washington Blvd., Stamford, CT   06901
(203) 659-3000 • fax: (203) 659-3001
e-mail: info@kab.org
website: www.kab.org

Founded in 1953, Keep America Beautiful is the nation's largest community improvement organization, focusing on the key issues of litter prevention, waste reduction/recycling, and community greening and beautification. The nonprofit group's "Great American Cleanup Day" draws nearly four million volunteers and participants nationwide each year for activities such as litter and illegal dumpsite clean-ups, park and trail maintenance, marine debris removal, recycling collections, tree plantings, community gardening, educational programs, and litter-free events. Meanwhile, the group's "America Recycles Day," held each year on November 15, is the only national community-driven awareness event to promote recycling in the United States. The Keep America Beautiful website offers a wide array of information about these and the group's many other initiatives, as well as in-depth reports such as the recent study "Recycling at Work."

## Natural Resources Defense Council (NRDC)
40 West 20th St., New York, NY   10011
(212) 727-2700 • fax: (212) 727-1773
e-mail: nrdcinfo@nrdc.org
website: www.nrdc.org

The Natural Resources Defense Council (NRDC) promotes the international protection of wildlife and wild places through law, science, and the activism of more than a million members. Some of the group's main focuses include climate change, alternative energy, and protection of the world's oceans and endangered habitats. The NRDC website offers in-depth information about a wide range of green practices and environmental topics and features scores of fact sheets, news items, and reports, as well as opportunities for individuals to get involved with its campaigns.

## Sierra Club
85 Second St., 2nd Floor, San Francisco, CA   94105
(415) 977-5500 • fax: (415) 977-5797
e-mail: information@sierraclub.org
website: www.sierraclub.org

One of the nation's oldest environmental organizations, the Sierra Club was founded in 1892 and has been working to protect and conserve the nation's environment ever since. The Sierra Club website features extensive information about green consumer practices, corporate greenwashing, environmental responsibility, and public policy analysis. Visitors to the site will also find the organization's policy statements, action alerts, blog posts, and in-depth articles from *Sierra*, the Club's bimonthly magazine.

## Union of Concerned Scientists (UCS)
2 Brattle Square, Cambridge, MA   02138-3780
(617) 547-5552 • fax: (617) 864-9405
website: www.ucsusa.org

The Union of Concerned Scientists (UCS) is a membership organization of citizens and scientists who work together to promote the responsible use of science to improve the world. UCS has extensively researched and reported on the impact of various green practices, such as sustainable agriculture, water conservation, biofuels and electric vehicles, compact florescent light bulbs, nuclear power, and alternative clean energy sources such as solar and wind. The group's website features a wide variety of reports, fact sheets, and public policy assessments. Publications available online include "Tomorrow's Clean Vehicles, Today (2015)," "The Natural Gas Gamble: A Risky Bet on America's Clean Energy Future," and a guide to so-called green consumer products, "Palm Oil Scorecard 2015: Fries, Face Wash, Forests." The UCS publishes a quarterly member newsletter, *Earthwise,* and also available for purchase from the site is the book *Cooler Smarter: Practical Steps for Low-Carbon Living.*

## US Environmental Protection Agency (EPA)
Office of Environmental Information 2810A
Washington, DC   20460
(202) 272-0167
website: www.epa.gov

The Environmental Protection Agency (EPA) is the federal government agency charged with ensuring that both human and environmental health in the United States are protected and preserved. With regional and specialized offices nationwide, the agency works to influence and promote positive environmental stewardship and policies. Established in 1970, the EPA leads the nation's environmental science, research, education, and assessment efforts. The agency's website includes a section devoted to "Greener Living," which features a good selection of information for consumers about green practices and their impacts.

## US Green Building Council (USGBC)
2101 L St. NW, Suite 500, Washington, DC   20037
(800) 795-1747
e-mail: leedinfo@usgbc.org
website: www.usgbc.org

The US Green Building Council (USGBC) is a diverse group of builders and environmentalists, corporations and nonprofits, teachers and students, lawmakers and citizens that share a vision of a sustainable built environment. Toward that end, the USGBC established LEED, the most widely recognized and widely used green building program in the world, certifying 1.5 million square feet of building space each day in 135 countries. LEED is a certification program that guides the design, construction, operations, and maintenance of buildings, homes, and communities. Today, more than fifty-four thousand projects are currently participating in LEED, comprising more than 10.1 billion square feet of construction space. The USGBC hosts an annual conference, "Greenbuild," and its website offers extensive information about green building innovations and trends as well as the LEED certification process and standards.

## Zero Waste America (ZWA)
217 South Jessup St., Philadelphia, PA   19107
(215) 629-3553
e-mail: lynnlandes@earthlink.net
website: www.zerowasteamerica.org

Zero Waste America (ZWA) is an Internet-based environmental research organization specializing in the field of "zero waste," a philosophy that encourages the reuse of products (and their components) throughout their lifecycles. ZWA specializes in information on US waste disposal issues, particularly the lack of a federal waste management plan, the use of disposal bans to legally stop waste disposal and imports, the long-proposed federal Interstate Waste legislation, waste data collection methodology, and applicable federal case law. Through its website, ZWA provides information on legislative, legal, technical, environmental, health, and consumer issues. Its website offers photos, analysis of successful and unsuccessful recycling plans, and links to sources of news about waste.

# Bibliography

## Books

Catherine Alexer and Joshua Reno — *Economies of Recycling: The Global Transformation of Materials, Values and Social Relations.* London: Zed Books, 2012.

Bart Barendregt and Rivke Jaffe, eds. — *Green Consumption: The Global Rise of Eco-Chic.* London: Bloomsbury Academic, 2014

Brian Clegg — *Eco-Logic: Cutting Through the Greenwash—Truth, Lies and Saving the Planet.* London: Eden Project, 2009.

Samantha MacBride — *Recycling Reconsidered: The Present Failure and Future Promise of Environmental Action in the United States.* Boston: MIT Press, 2013.

William McDonough — *The Upcycle: Beyond Sustainability—Designing for Abundance.* New York: North Point, 2013.

Adam Minter — *Junkyard Planet: Travels in the Billion-Dollar Trash Trade.* London: Bloomsbury, 2013.

Margo Oge — *Driving the Future: Combating Climate Change with Cleaner, Smarter Cars.* New York: Arcade, 2015.

Guy Pearse  *The Greenwash Effect: Corporate Deception, Celebrity Environmentalists, and What Big Business Isn't Telling You About Their Green Products and Brands.* New York: Skyhorse, 2014.

Jeremy Shere  *Renewable: The World-Changing Power of Alternative Energy.* New York: St. Martin's Press, 2013.

Seth Shulman et al.  *Cooler Smarter: Practical Steps for Low-Carbon Living.* Washington, DC: Island Press, 2012.

## Periodicals and Internet Sources

Jonathan Amos  "'Next Pinatubo' a Test of Geoengineering," *BBC Science*, February 15, 2015. www.bbc.com.

Jonathan Bardelline  "Why Bottle Recycling in US Is Still Just a Drop in the Bucket," GreenBiz, August 11, 2011. www.greenbiz.com.

D. Burdick  "Top 10 Greenwashing Companies in America," *Huffington Post*, April 3, 2009. www.huffingtonpost.com.

Sean Cockerham  "Lawmaker: Protect Coal Plants to Help the Manatees," *Miami Herald*, March 20, 2015.

Juriah Conding et al.  "A Review: The Impacts of Green Practices Adoption on Performance in the Malaysian Automotive Industry," *Journal of Sustainable Development Studies*, January 2013.

Environmental          "Overview of Greenhouse Gases,"
Protection Agency   2014. www.epa.gov.

Matt Ewadinger      "Recycling Creates Jobs and Boosts
and Scott Mouw      Economy," *BioCycle*, October 2005.
                            www.biocycle.net.

Jesse Finfrock and   "Pouring Biofuel on the Fire:
Nichole Wong         Hunger. Corruption. Bankruptcy.
                            Other than That, the Green-Fuel
                            Boom Has Been a Smashing Success,"
                            *Mother Jones*, March/April 2009.

Fox News               "Are Compact Fluorescent Light
                            Bulbs Good for the Environment?,"
                            November 8, 2007.
                            www.foxnews.com.

Mike Gaworecki     "Biofuels Are Bad News for Forests,
                            Climate, Food Security, Says Report,"
                            mongabay.com, February 27, 2015.
                            http://news.mongabay.com.

Richard Gray and   "Energy Saving Light Bulbs Offer
Julia McWatt          Dim Future," *Telegraph* (UK), August
                            29, 2009.

Green Dashboard   "Waste Diverted from Landfills," July
                            13, 2012.
                            https://greendashboard.dc.gov.

Lynn Grooms          "Biodiesel Industry Turns to Corn
                            Oil," *Farm Industry News*, April 29,
                            2014.

Eric Hagerman        "Little Green Lies—How Companies
                            Erect an Eco-Façade," *Wired*, October
                            20, 2008.

Hannah Hoag and Nature — "Price on Carbon Failing to Reduce Greenhouse Gas Emissions," *Scientific American*, November 28, 2011.

Don Hofstrand — "The Impact of Biofuels on Agriculture," *AgMRC Renewable Energy Newsletter*, June 2008. www.agmrc.org.

EunHa Jeonga et al. — "The Impact of Eco-Friendly Practices on Green Image and Customer Attitudes: An Investigation in a Café Setting," *International Journal of Hospitality Management*, August 2014.

Jonathan Klick and Joshua D. Wright — "Grocery Bag Bans and Foodborne Illness," Social Science Research Network, November 2, 2012. http://ssrn.com.

Kim Krisberg — "Green Workplace Practices Making an Impact on Health: Public Health Workers Leading by Example," Medscape, 2008. www.medscape.com.

Veronique LaCapra — "With 'Single-Stream' Recycling, Convenience Comes at a Cost," National Public Radio. March 31, 2015. www.npr.org.

Miguel Llanos — "Plastic Bottles Pile up as Mountains of Waste—Americans' Thirst for Portable Water Is Behind Drop in Recycling Rate," NBC News, March 3, 2005. www.nbcnews.com.

Larisa Manescu — "Don't Misunderstand Plastic Bags' Impact," *Daily Texan*, February 19, 2013.

Jeff McMahon — "Lower Carbon = Higher Profit," *Forbes*, April 16, 2015.

Cahal Milmo — "Electronic Waste Worth £34bn Piling up in 'Toxic Mine', Warns UN Report," *Independent* (UK), April 19, 2015.

Julian Morris — "Your Whole Foods Tote Could Be More Harmful than a Plastic Bag," *Time*, August 5, 2014.

Ralph Nader — "Seeking Sustainability," *Huffington Post*, May 10, 2013. www.huffingtonpost.com.

Tamaryn Napp, Nilay Shah, and David Fisk — "What's Energy Efficiency and How Much Can It Help Cut Emissions?," *Guardian* (UK), June 8, 2012.

Natural Resources Defense Council — "Eat Green: Our Everyday Food Choices Affect Global Warming and the Environment," 2012. www.nrdc.org.

Natural Resources Defense Council — "Grasping Green Car Technology," 2015. www.nrdc.org.

New Jersey WasteWise Business Network — "The Economic Benefits of Recycling—WasteWise Case Studies from the Private and Public Sectors," 2013. www.nj.gov.

Barrett Newkirk          "Eww, Reusable Grocery Bags' Germs
                         Can Make You Sick," *Desert Sun*,
                         January 6, 2014.

Fred Pearce              "Greenwash: Why 'Clean Coal' Is the
                         Ultimate Climate-Change
                         Oxymoron," *Guardian* (UK),
                         February 26, 2009.

William Pentland         "Big Corn Gets Bigger: America's
                         Ethanol Decade," *Forbes*, August 22,
                         2011.

Steven Rinaldi           "Economic Benefits of Recycling,"
                         New Jersey Department of
                         Environmental Protection, Division
                         of Solid and Hazardous Waste,
                         January 13, 2014. www.state.nj.us.

Elizabeth                "Biofuels Deemed a Greenhouse
Rosenthal                Threat," *New York Times*, February 8,
                         2008.

Jean-Louis Santini       "Scientists Seek International
                         Authority on Climate
                         Geoengineering," Yahoo! News,
                         February 15, 2015.
                         http://news.yahoo.com.

Satish Sinha et al.      "Impact of E-Waste Recycling on
                         Water and Soil," Toxics Link, 2014.
                         http://toxicslink.org.

E.E. Smith and S.        "A Perceptual Study of the Impact of
Perks                    Green Practice Implementation on
                         the Business Functions," *Southern
                         African Business Review*, vol. 14, no.
                         3, 2010. www.unisa.ac.za.

Tellus Institute      "More Jobs, Less Pollution: Growing
and Sound             the Recycling Economy in the US,"
Resource              Natural Resources Defense Council,
Management            2011. http://docs.nrdc.org.

Julia Whitty          "The Dark Side of Biofuels," *Mother
                      Jones*, February 11, 2008.

Stiv Wilson           "In Defense of Plastic Bag Bans,"
                      *Huffington Post*, February 28, 2012.
                      www.huffingtonpost.com.

# Index

CPSIA information can be obtained
at www.ICGtesting.com
Printed in the USA
FFOW05n1847060216